Englisch

ABSCHLUSS-PRÜFUNGS-TRAINER

Mittlerer Schulabschluss
Hessen

Abschlussprüfungstrainer Englisch
Mittlerer Schulabschluss | Hessen

Illustrationen
Cornelsen / Karen Donnelly 2017: (S. 22, S. 23, S. 36, S. 38, S. 41, S. 60)

Bildquellen
akg-images A.P.L. (S. 20 *oben:* New Line Cinema); **akg-images** (S. 46: Fototeca Gilardi); **Fotolia** (S. 14 *unten:* essevu, S. 18 *oben:* Axel Bueckert, S. 18 Mitte: Rido, S. 18 *unten:* snowwhiteimages, S. 29: Africa Studio, S. 57 *oben:* corlaffra, S. 65: JavaJunkie); **Glow Images** (S. 35: Fancy); **mauritius images** (S. 15: Penny Tweedie/Alamy Stock Photo, S. 14 *oben:* Photo 12/Alamy Stock Photo); **Shutterstock** (S. 9: Jeff Whyte, S. 10: Mikhail Kolesnikov, S. 13: Constantin Stanciu, S. 20 *unten:* sherpa, S. 25: mubus7, S. 28: Evocation Images, S. 38: fizkes, S. 44 *oben:* David Pickett, S. 44 *unten:* SUNDAYUA, S. 47: Rawpixel.com, S. 48: Dragan Jovanovic, S. 51: View Apart, S. 55: Photomika-com, S. 56: Andrey Nikulin, S. 57 *unten:* Katariina Järvinen, S. 62: Nolte Lourens, S. 68 *alle:* Goxy, S. 71: Alp Aksoy)

Erarbeitet von: Gwen Berwick, York; Sydney Thorne, York
In Zusammenarbeit mit der Englischredaktion: Klaus Unger (Projektleitung)
Ingrid Raspe (verantwortliche Redakteurin)
Illustrationen: Karen Donnelly, Brighton
Layout-Konzept: Klein & Halm Grafikdesign, Berlin
Umschlaggestaltung: Agentur Rosendahl, Berlin
Layout und technische Umsetzung: Klein & Halm Grafikdesign, Berlin

www.cornelsen.de

1. Auflage, 1. Druck 2017

© 2017 Cornelsen Verlag GmbH, Berlin

Druck: H. Heenemann, Berlin

ISBN 978-3-06-034858-9

PEFC zertifiziert
Dieses Produkt stammt aus nachhaltig
bewirtschafteten Wäldern und kontrollierten
Quellen.
www.pefc.de

PEFC/04-31-1156

Inhaltsverzeichnis

Vorwort

Training Section

Hörverstehen – *Listening comprehension*

Leseverstehen – *Reading comprehension*

Sprachgebrauch – *Use of language*

Schreiben – *Text production*

Musterprüfungen

Lösungen (als Einleger in der Mitte des Heftes)

Was erwartet dich in der Abschlussarbeit?

Liebe Schülerin, lieber Schüler,

bald ist es für dich so weit und du legst die zentrale Prüfung im Fach Englisch ab. Damit du weißt, was auf dich zukommt, wollen wir dir genau erklären, was dich in der Prüfung erwartet und wie du dich optimal vorbereiten kannst.

Die zentrale Abschlussarbeit Englisch im Überblick

Die zentrale Abschlussarbeit besteht aus vier Teilen. Zunächst hast du 15 Minuten Zeit, dir die Arbeit durchzuschauen, dich zu orientieren und noch einmal 15 Minuten, um eventuelle allgemeine Fragen zu stellen. Danach beginnt mit dem Abspielen der Hörtexte die Bearbeitungszeit von 135 Minuten.

	Kompetenz	Ausgangstexte und Aufgaben	Zeit	Punkte

Teil A	Hörverstehen	• zwei bis vier Hörtexte (z.B. Reportage, Dialog, Interview)
		 • verschiedene Aufgabenformate:
		   – Auswahlaufgaben *(Multiple choice)*
		   – Zuordnungsaufgaben *(Matching)*
		   – Kurzantwort-Aufgaben *(Giving short answers)*
			135 Minuten + 15 Minuten Einarbeitungszeit + 15 Minuten Zeit für allgemeine Fragen	25 Punkte

Teil B	Leseverstehen	• drei Lesetexte
		 • verschiedene Aufgabenformate:
		   – Zuordnungsaufgaben *(Multiple choice)*
		   – Auswahlaufgaben *(Matching)*
		   – Kurzantwort-Aufgaben *(Giving short answers)*
				25 Punkte

Teil C	Sprachgebrauch	• Mediation: Vermitteln auf der Basis eines Textes/Dialogs, Notizen auf Englisch verfassen
		 • Words and structures:
		   – Einsetzaufgabe *(Fill the gap)*
		   – Auswahlaufgaben *(Multiple choice)*
				25 Punkte

Teil D	Schreiben	• Auswahl zwischen 2 Aufgaben: kreatives Schreiben entweder mit Bildimpuls oder nach Vorgabe eines Themas (150 Wörter)		25 Punkte

Hilfsmittel in der Prüfung

Während der schriftlichen Prüfung sind zweisprachige Wörterbücher erlaubt, elektronische Wörterbücher dürfen jedoch nicht verwendet werden.
Du findest in diesem Heft aber auch Übungen und Tipps, die dir helfen, unbekannte Wörter und Aussagen zu entschlüsseln. Mach dir gleichzeitig bewusst, dass du nicht jedes einzelne Wort kennen musst, um einen Text in seinen wichtigsten Aussagen zu verstehen.

Die vier Teile der Abschlussprüfung

Hörverstehen – *Listening comprehension*

Im ersten Teil der Abschlussarbeit hörst du mehrere verschiedene Hörtexte, zu denen du Aufgaben lösen musst. Vor dem Abspielen der Hörtexte hast du Zeit, dich mit den Aufgaben vertraut zu machen. In diesem Prüfungsteil erwarten dich folgende Aufgabentypen:
*   Auswahlaufgaben (*Multiple choice*)
*   Zuordnungsaufgaben (*Matching*)
*   Einsetzaufgaben (*Fill the gaps*)
*   Kurzantwort-Aufgaben (*Giving short answers*)

Leseverstehen – *Reading comprehension*

Der zweite Teil der Prüfung umfasst mehrere Texte zum Lesen – das können Sachtexte sein oder literarische Texte. Anhand von Aufgaben musst du zeigen, dass du die Texte verstanden hast.
Beim Leseverstehen können folgende Aufgabentypen vorkommen:
*   Auswahlaufgaben (*Multiple choice*)
*   Fragen beantworten (*Answer the questions*)
*   Zuordnungsaufgaben (*Matching*)

Manchmal bekommst du den Hinweis
*   *You cannot find the answer to the following question directly in the text:*
    Dann findest du die Antwort nur indirekt im Text. Es hilft dir z.B., wenn du dich in die Personen im Text hineinversetzt und dich fragst, wie sie sich wohl in der beschriebenen Situation fühlen.

Sprachgebrauch – *Use of language*

Dieser Prüfungsteil besteht aus zwei Unter-Abschnitten:
Mediation (Sprachmittlung) und **Words and structures** (Wortschatz und Grammatik).

Bei der **Mediation** wird eine Situation beschrieben, in der du zwischen deutsch- und englischsprachigen Sprecherinnen und Sprechern vermittelst. Basis können Dialoge oder Texte sein. Dabei sollst du nicht Wort für Wort übersetzen, sondern die wichtigen Informationen in deinen eigenen Worten übertragen. Dann liest du einen deutschen oder englischen Text, z.B. eine Informationsbroschüre, und gibst die wichtigsten Punkte, angeleitet durch Fragen, in der anderen Sprache wieder.

Im Bereich **Words and structures** erwarten dich Aufgaben des Typs
*   Lückentext mit Wortspeicher (*Banked gap-filling*)
*   Auswahlaufgaben (*Multiple choice*)

Schreiben – *Text production*

Im vierten und letzten Teil der schriftlichen Prüfung bekommst du zwei Themen zur Auswahl, z.B. ein vorgegebenes Foto oder einen kurzen Satz/eine Überschrift, von denen du dich für eines entscheiden musst. Wenn du dich entschieden hast, schreibst du einen zusammenhängenden Text in einer Länge von ca. 150 Wörtern (z.B. Tagebucheintrag, Brief oder E-Mail, Bericht oder Kommentar, Argumentation, Zusammenfassung oder eine selbst erlebte oder erfundene Geschichte).

Wie arbeitest du mit diesem Heft?

In diesem Heft lernst du durch gezielte Übungen, wie du die Aufgaben zu allen Prüfungsteilen bearbeiten kannst. Darüber hinaus bekommst du konkrete Prüfungsbeispiele. Das Heft ist deshalb wie folgt aufgebaut:

Das **erste Kapitel**, die *Training Section*, gliedert sich in die fünf Kompetenzbereiche, die in der zentralen Abschlussarbeit geprüft werden: Hörverstehen, Leseverstehen, Sprachgebrauch und Schreiben.
Die *Training Section* enthält:

- Hinweise zum Ablauf und zur Bewertung jedes einzelnen Kompetenzbereichs,
- Beispiele und Tipps für alle Aufgabenformate, die in der Prüfung vorkommen können, also *Multiple choice*, *Matching* etc.,
- zahlreiche Strategien zum Umgang mit typischen Schwierigkeiten, wie z. B. Verständnisproblemen,
- vielfältige Aufgaben zum Üben deines Hör- und Leseverständnisses sowie deiner Wortschatzkenntnisse.

> **Tipp**
>
> Blau umrandete Felder markieren Tipps, die dir bei den Aufgaben helfen.

Es empfiehlt sich, die *Training Section* als erstes durchzuarbeiten, und zwar Kompetenzbereich für Kompetenzbereich. So verschaffst du dir einen Überblick darüber, was du schon gut kannst, wo du noch üben solltest und welche Strategien dir dabei helfen.

Das **zweite Kapitel** bietet dir zwei komplette **Musterprüfungen**, die jeweils alle vier Kompetenzbereiche (Hörverstehen, Leseverstehen, Sprachgebrauch, Schreiben) enthalten. Sie sind den Prüfungen der letzten Jahre nachempfunden. Du lernst dadurch Schritt für Schritt die gesamte Prüfungssituation und den Aufbau einer Prüfung kennen.

Wenn du feststellst, dass du mit einem Kompetenzbereich oder einem Aufgabenformat noch Schwierigkeiten hast, gehe zurück in die *Training Section* und wiederhole gezielt die entsprechenden Übungen und Strategien oder nutze die Online-Übungen zu Grammatik und Wortschatz auf www.scook.de.

Die **Tonaufnahmen und Hörtexte** für die *Training Section* und die Musterprüfungen findest du ebenfalls online unter www.scook.de. Das Kopfhörer-Symbol mit Track-Nummer im Heft zeigt dir an, welchen Hörtext du für die Aufgabe anhören musst.

Mit dem **Lösungsteil** in der Mitte des Heftes kannst du deine Ergebnisse überprüfen und – wenn nötig – verbessern. Dort findest du auch eine Tabelle zur Benotung.

Nützliche Tipps zur Prüfungsvorbereitung erhältst du auf S. 42.

Nun kannst du zuversichtlich sein, dass du weißt, was in der zentralen Prüfung auf dich zukommt, und dass du die unterschiedlichen Aufgabenstellungen geübt hast und kennst.

> Zusätzlich kannst du dein Grundwissen in den Bereichen Grammatik und Wortschatz mithilfe von Online-Übungen wiederholen und vertiefen. Nutze dazu den Zugangscode auf Seite 1 (www.scook.de).
>
> Ebenfalls online findest du die Tonaufnahmen zu den Höraufgaben als MP3-Downloads, die Hörtexte sowie die Originalprüfungen früherer Jahre mit Lösungen. Nutze dazu ebenfalls den Code von Seite 1.

Viel Spaß beim Training mit diesem Heft und viel Erfolg bei der Prüfung!

ABSCHLUSS-
PRÜFUNGS-
TRAINER

Hessen

Training Section

Hörverstehen – *Listening comprehension*

1. Ablauf und Bewertung der Abschlussarbeit

Die Prüfung

Die **schriftliche Prüfung** besteht aus **Hörverstehen**, **Leseverstehen**, **Mediating**, **Word and structures** und **Text production** (Schreiben). Für alle Teile zusammen hast du 135 Minuten Zeit. Zusätzlich erhältst du vorab 15 Minuten Zeit, die du verwenden kannst, um dir einen Überblick über die Aufgaben zu verschaffen und zu schauen, ob dir alles klar ist. Danach können 15 Minuten lang allgemeine Fragen gestellt werden.

Ablauf beim Hörverstehen

Beim **Hörverstehen** hörst du zunächst zwei kurze Hörtexte. Dazu gibt es Auswahlaufgaben *(Multiple choice)*. Dann hörst du zwei längere Hörtexte, z.B. Interviews. Dazu gibt es z.B. eine Zuordnungsaufgabe *(Matching)*, bei der du die Sprecher einer Auswahl an Aussagen zuordnen musst, und eine Kurzantwort-Aufgabe *(Giving short answers)*, bei der du in deinen eigenen Worten Fragen beantwortest.
Du hörst alle Hörtexte zweimal. Du hast zunächst 30 Sekunden Zeit, um die Aufgaben zu lesen. Dann hörst du den Hörtext zum ersten Mal. Du bearbeitest die Aufgaben und hörst anschließend den Hörtext noch ein zweites Mal. Dies ist das Vorgehen bei allen Texten der Prüfung.

Bewertung beim Hörverstehen

Ein zweisprachiges Wörterbuch ist erlaubt. Elektronische Wörterbücher dürfen aber nicht verwendet werden. Du brauchst aber keine Angst vor Grammatik- oder Rechtschreibfehlern in deinen Antworten zu haben. Solange man versteht, was du geschrieben hast, gehen sie in diesem Prüfungsteil nicht in die Bewertung ein. Das Hörverstehen macht 25% der Abschlussarbeit aus.

2. Typische Aufgabenformate in Hessen

In diesem Kapitel lernst du die typischen Aufgabenformate kennen, die dich bei der Abschlussarbeit im Bereich Hörverstehen erwarten. Die blauen Kästen enthalten nützliche Strategien, wie du mit häufigen Schwierigkeiten umgehen kannst.

Calgary's skyways

You are going to hear five parts of a radio interview about the skyway network in Calgary, a city in western Canada.

1 Auswahlaufgaben *(Multiple choice)*

1

> - *First read the task.*
> - *Then listen to the interview.*
> - *While you are listening, tick (✓) the correct box.*
> - *At the end you will hear the interview again.*

Tipp

Bei *Multiple choice*-Aufgaben werden einzelne Wörter aus dem Hörtext häufig ersetzt durch:
Synonyme:
climate im Hörtext   = *weather* in Antwort **C**

Gegensätze:
exposed to (the climate) ≠ *avoid (the weather)*
im Hörtext   in Antwort **C**
(dem Klima) ausgesetzt   (das Wetter) vermeiden

An underground city ...

A ☐ is a famous tourist site in Calgary.

B ☐ can be very cold.

C ☐ allows people to avoid the cold weather.

2 Zuordnungsaufgaben *(Matching)*

🎧 2

- *First read the task.*
- *You will now hear more about the Skyways, and what the word Skyways means in different parts of North America. What does Skyways mean in these five places? Look at the definitions. There is one more definition than you need.*
- *Listen to the interview twice.*

Overhead pedestrian passage in Calgary

Tipp

Die Wörter in den Definitionen kommen im Hörtext nicht vor. Überlege dir also im Voraus, was für Wörter vorkommen könnten. In B geht es um ein Kino. Achte im Hörtext also auf Begriffe wie *movie*, *watch*, *open air* oder *theatre*.

A	B	C
a company that flies planes	an outdoor cinema	a restaurant at the top of a high-rise building

D	E	F
part of the road system	a see-through walkway for tourists	part of the public transport system

1 Burlington: _____

2 Stoney Creek: _____

3 Kissimmee: _____

4 Jacksonville: _____

5 Jasper National Park: _____

3 Einsetzaufgaben *(Fill in the gap)*

🎧 3

- *First read the tasks (1–2).*
- *Then listen to the third part of the interview.*
- *While you are listening, fill in the information.*
- *At the end you will hear the interview again.*

1 Calgary has a system of _____

passageways 15 feet up in the air.

Tipp

Denke an den Sinn der fehlenden Wörter. Die *passageways* sind in der Luft, **über deinem Kopf** ...

2 There are passageways between buildings all over

_____ Calgary.

4 Kurzantwort-Aufgaben *(Giving short answers)*

> • *First read the tasks (1–2).*
> • *Then listen to the fourth part of the interview and answer the questions.*
> • *At the end you will hear the interview again.*

1 What are **two** advantages for pedestrians?

A _____

B _____ (2 points)

2 Why do some people criticize the skyways?

_____ (1 point)

Tipp

• Bei diesem Aufgabentyp sollst du die Antworten in deinen eigenen Worten geben. Du brauchst nicht Wort für Wort aus dem Hörtext zu zitieren.

• Bei Fragen mit zwei Punkten musst du zwei verschiedene Antworten geben, um die volle Punktzahl zu erreichen.

5 Richtig/Falsch-Aufgaben *(True/False)*

> • *First read the task.*
> • *Then listen to the fifth part of the interview and tick (✓) the correct box.*
> • *At the end you will hear the interview again.*

1 Over 22,000 people use the busiest bridge every weekend.

This statement is …   ☐ true   ☐ false

2 Harold Hanen was born in Calgary.

This statement is …   ☐ true   ☐ false

3 He did some of his studies abroad.

This statement is …   ☐ true   ☐ false

Tipp

• Vorsicht in Sätzen mit Zahlen: Achte nicht nur auf die Zahl, sondern auch auf den Rest des Satzes, z. B. *every weekend* in **Satz 1**.

• Achte auch auf **Synonyme**, z. B. *a native of* im Hörtext = *born in* in **Satz 2**.

3. Umgang mit Verständnisproblemen

Die Hörtexte in der Abschlussprüfung enthalten manchmal Wörter, die du nicht kennst oder die du beim ersten oder zweiten Hören nicht verstehst. Das ist ganz normal. Also keine Panik – es gibt Strategien, die dir helfen, die wesentlichen Inhalte trotzdem zu erfassen und die Aufgabe zu lösen. In diesem Kapitel werden anhand eines Werbefilms über die Niagarafälle die wichtigsten Strategien vorgestellt.

The Niagara Falls

The following text is the audio track of a publicity film about the Niagara Falls.

> • *First read the tasks (1–5).*
> • *Then listen to the programme. You can read the text while you listen.*
> • *Do tasks 1–5: tick (✓) the correct box or fill in the information.*
> • *At the end you will hear the text again (task 6).*

Tipp

Die Tonaufnahme (Track 6) enthält Störgeräusche, die einige Textstellen unverständlich machen. Im Hörtext sind diese Stellen durch Schwärzungen kenntlich gemacht. Dieses Vorgehen soll dir verdeutlichen, dass du einige der Aufgaben 1–5 trotz der fehlenden Textstellen lösen kannst. Bei anderen Aufgaben kannst du mithilfe der Tipps zumindest Vermutungen anstellen.

Beim zweiten Hören (Track 7) in Aufgabe 6 hörst du den Text ohne Störgeräusche. Nun kannst du überprüfen, ob deine Vermutungen richtig waren.

Welcome to the Niagara Falls! These astonishing natural waterfalls are on the border between the USA and Canada. They consist of three waterfalls. The two smaller ones are in the
5 USA. But these amazing falls, called the Horseshoe Falls, are the biggest and they're ▓▓▓ in Canada. The Niagara Falls are located near important urban centres. It only takes half an hour by car to get to Buffalo.

10 These tourists have just landed at Buffalo International Airport and they're on their way to see the famous falls. In fact, about 30 million people visit the Niagara Falls each year! This group is going on the very popular *Maid of the*
15 *Mist* tour – a boat tour to the bottom of the waterfalls. The air here is full of ▓▓▓▓▓ ▓▓▓▓▓ – that's why everyone here is wearing ▓▓▓▓▓. But don't be fooled – most of them are going to get wet anyway. Oh!
20 Here comes the next shower!

Accessing the falls is easy. That's great because it means that thousands of people can come and see the fantastic sight. But it also means that the falls have to be well protected
25 and taken care of. In fact, these falls on the American side are actually part of ▓▓▓▓▓ ▓▓▓ state park. It was designed by the same man who laid out this well-known park. Do you recognize it? It's Central Park in New York City. Luckily state parks don't charge entrance – 30 so you don't have to pay to see the falls. Tourists can stand right next to the top of the Horseshoe Falls and watch the water spilling over. Isn't it amazing?

Sometimes people have gone over the falls. 35 Some have even done it by choice. This is Annie Taylor – she was the first person to ride over the Niagara Falls, way back in 1901, on her 63rd birthday. After her husband and son had died, Annie was facing poverty and decided to go 40 over the falls ▓▓▓▓▓. And guess what she used to cross the falls: this thing. That's right – a wooden barrel. The sort of barrel that was used to store wine or beer. Crazy, isn't it? She put cushions and a mattress inside and asked some 45 friends to push the barrel in the right direction at the top – and other friends to open it when she got to the bottom of the falls. And she did: she went over the top of the falls, the barrel fell, and when her friends opened it, she was alive. 50 But although Annie (amazingly!) came out with no broken bones, she ▓▓▓▓▓: it was bleeding. After her crazy experiment, Annie warned other people against doing the same thing. We'll take your advice, Annie. 55

1 The Horseshoe Falls …

A ☐ are smaller than the American falls.

B ☐ are fully in Canada.

C ☐ are for the most part in Canada.

Tipp

Wenn du nicht gleich auf die richtige Antwort kommst, wende das Ausschlussverfahren an:
- Markiere die Stelle im ersten Absatz, die Antwort A ausschließt.
- Zwischen B und C kannst du dich noch nicht entscheiden: Im Hörtext könnte es nämlich heißen **only** in Canada, **mainly** in Canada, **partly** in Canada oder **fully** in Canada.

Also wirst du nochmals hören müssen. Aber jetzt kannst du gezielt zwischen zwei möglichen Antworten entscheiden – das ist leichter als zwischen dreien.

2 The people on the boat tours need protection. Give **one** example of how they protect themselves.

Tipp

Hier kannst du dir helfen, indem du Vermutungen anstellst:
- Die Touristen sind laut Hörtext *wet* (= nass).
- Wie kann man sich gegen Nässe schützen? Zu erwarten sind also Wörter wie *raincoat, umbrella, waterproof* etc.

Achte beim zweiten Zuhören besonders gut auf diese Stelle. Mit dieser Vorbereitung wirst du sie bestimmt besser verstehen.

3 The land on the American side of the falls …

A ☐ can only be reached if you pay.

B ☐ was the first state park in the USA.

C ☐ looks like Central Park in New York City.

Tipp

Wende das Ausschlussverfahren an!
Lösung C kannst du sogar, wenn du fast nichts verstanden hast, mit dem gesunden Menschenverstand ausschließen. Warum?

Lösung A kannst du ebenfalls ausschließen, wenn du die relevante Stelle im Text verstanden hast. Markiere diese Stelle.

4 Annie Taylor went over the falls in a barrel in

order to _____ .

Tipp

Was weißt du über Annie Taylor? Kannst du daraus schließen, zu welchem Zweck sie so etwas Gefährliches gemacht hat?

5 When Annie Taylor's friends opened the barrel, they found that she was …

A ☐ dead.

B ☐ injured.

C ☐ unhurt.

Tipp

• Markiere das Wort im Hörtext, mit dem du Lösung A ausschließen kannst.
• Das Wort *although* (= obwohl) im Text leitet einen Gegensatz ein: Obwohl sie nichts gebrochen hatte, war sie _____ .
Dank dieses Wortes kannst du also beim zweiten Hören zwischen Lösung B und Lösung C wählen. Siehst du wie?

• *Now read tasks 6 and 7.*
• *Then listen to the programme again. This time it's complete.*
• *Do task 6 while you are listening.*
• *Then do task 7.*

6 Listen to the complete programme. Note the exact words in the recording.

A … the Horseshoe Falls are the biggest and they're _____ in Canada.

B … everyone here is wearing _____ .

C … these falls on the American side are actually part of _____ state park.

D Annie (…) decided to go over the falls to _____ .

E But although Annie (amazingly!) came out with no broken bones, she _____

_____ – it was bleeding.

7 Now use your information from task 6 to check your answers to tasks 1–5.

4. Hörverstehen – *Now you*

In diesem Kapitel kannst du die Strategien, die du auf den letzten Seiten kennen gelernt hast, bei ausge-wählten Aufgaben zum Hörverstehen gezielt üben. Grundlage dafür sind ein Dialog über ein Radrennen in Yorkshire sowie ein Radio-Interview über die jamaikanische Reggae-Legende Bob Marley.

Auswahlaufgaben *(Multiple choice)*

The Tour de Yorkshire

Sarah from Ireland and Mo from Yorkshire are talking about a cycling race in Yorkshire. You will hear their telephone conversation.

8

> • *First read the tasks.*
> • *Then listen to the dialogue.*
> • *While you are listening, tick (✓) the correct box.*
> • *At the end you will hear the dialogue again.*
> • *Now read the tasks. You have 90 seconds to do this.*

Yellow bicycle on the city walls of York, 2014

1 In 2014 the *Tour de France* cycling race ...

A ☐ began in France and came to Yorkshire.

B ☐ went through other countries and then came to Yorkshire.

C ☐ began in Yorkshire.

2 During the stages of the race in Yorkshire ...

A ☐ cycling fans rode yellow bicycles on the sides of the roads used by the race.

B ☐ people bought lots of yellow bicycles.

C ☐ there were old yellow bicycles on the sides of the roads used by the race.

3 The organizers of the *Tour de France* ...

A ☐ planned for large crowds.

B ☐ did not expect the enthusiastic reaction from people in Yorkshire.

C ☐ hoped that many people would join the cyclists.

4 The *Tour de France* ...

A ☐ was in Yorkshire for 21 days.

B ☐ left people in Yorkshire wanting to see more cycling races.

C ☐ went from Yorkshire directly on to France.

5 The *Tour de Yorkshire* cycling race ...

A ☐ includes hills that are difficult even for experienced cyclists.

B ☐ uses wide roads to allow for big groups of cyclists to pass through.

C ☐ has become a very popular off-road race.

Richtig/Falsch-Aufgaben *(True/False)*

Bob Marley

Radio presenter Joshua Needham is talking to Reggae expert Gwen Devlin about the Jamaican singer-songwriter Bob Marley.

Bob Marley (1945–1981)

> • *Listen to the interview.*
> • *Decide whether each sentence is true or false.*
> • *Put a tick (✓) in the correct box 'true' or 'false'.*
> • *You will hear the interview twice.*

		true	false
1	Bob Marley's dad was much older than his wife.	☐	☐
2	Kingston was an important place for Bob Marley's musical life.	☐	☐
3	Fans agree that Bob Marley's early song *Simmer Down* was his best song.	☐	☐
4	In a shooting incident, Marley's wife was killed.	☐	☐
5	In England, Bob Marley became a songwriter.	☐	☐
6	Bob Marley was a controversial figure because he took drugs.	☐	☐
7	When Bob Marley discovered he had cancer, he flew straight back to Jamaica.	☐	☐
8	Bob Marley died in Jamaica.	☐	☐

Notizen anfertigen *(Note-taking)*

Top of the Rock

You are on a visit to New York City, and you hear this radio advert for the *Top of the Rock* Observation Deck.

> • *Listen to the advert.*
> • *Complete the notes by filling the gaps B–G.*
> • *You will hear the recording twice.*
> • *The first question is an example.*

View from *Top of the Rock* Observation Deck

Number of floors up:	**A**	70
Great views of buildings and …	**B**	
Opens at:	**C**	
Advantage of online tickets:	**D**	
Price for 16-year-olds:	**E**	
Advantage of Sun and Stars tickets:	**F**	
Tip for night visits:	**G**	

Leseverstehen – *Reading comprehension*

1. Ablauf und Bewertung der Abschlussarbeit

Der zweite Prüfungsteil ist das **Leseverstehen**. In diesem Teil der Abschlussarbeit liest du drei Texte und zu jedem Text gibt es eine Aufgabe.

Ein zweisprachiges Wörterbuch ist erlaubt. Elektronische Wörterbücher dürfen aber nicht verwendet werden. Bei deinen Antworten werden Rechtschreib- und Grammatikfehler nur dann bewertet, wenn man nicht mehr verstehen kann, was du geschrieben hast.

Das Leseverstehen macht 25% deiner Gesamtnote aus.

2. Typische Aufgabenformate in Hessen

Im Folgenden lernst du die typischen Textsorten und Aufgabentypen kennen, die dich bei der Abschlussarbeit im Bereich Leseverstehen erwarten.

Die Tipp-Kästen enthalten nützliche Strategien, um mit typischen Schwierigkeiten umzugehen.

Australia's Stolen Generations

- *First read the text from a museum about Aboriginal people in Australia.*
- *Exercises 1–4 refer to this text.*

1 In the late nineteenth and early twentieth centuries the Australian government adopted the policy of taking Aboriginal children away from their homes – even if the parents tried to resist.

2 This was the fate of over 250,000 Aboriginal children, some say as many as 500,000, who had to leave their parents.

Aboriginal child in Australia

3 The children from Aboriginal families were housed in new English-speaking homes where they were not allowed to speak their own language. And they were given the typical foods of white Australians, even though they weren't used to it.

4 The parents were not told where their children were, and the children were not allowed to get in touch with their parents. The result was that the children had no contact with their families, their language, their music and their former way of life.

1 Den Textteilen Überschriften zuordnen *(Find the correct headings)*

> • *Match the four correct headings to the parts of the text (1–4). Be careful – there is one heading more than you need.*

A   A DIFFERENT LIFE

B   FORCED REMOVAL

C   FAMILIES

D   LARGE NUMBERS

E   ISOLATED

> **Tipp**
>
> Vorsicht bei gleichen Wörtern! Das Wort **families** kommt in Absatz **4** und Überschrift C vor – aber C passt trotzdem nicht zu Absatz **4**.
> Was hilft dir?
> • **Synonyme** (Wörter mit ähnlicher Bedeutung), zum Beispiel:
>   B) Removal – take away (Absatz **1**)
>   E) Isolated – no contact (Absatz **4**)
> • **Sammelbegriffe**, die stellvertretend für Beispiele im Text verwendet werden. Zum Beispiel:
>   D) Large numbers – 250 000, 500 000 (Absatz **2**)
>   A) A different life – new home, new language, new food (Absatz **3**)

part of the text	1	2	3	4
heading				

2 Auswahlaufgaben *(Multiple choice)*

> • *Read paragraphs 1 and 2 again.*
> • *Then tick (✓) the right statements. There is only one possible answer per statement.*

1   What happened to thousands of Aboriginal children?

A ☐ They died of disease.

B ☐ They were removed from their parents.

C ☐ They were forced to stay with their parents.

D ☐ They wanted to leave their parents.

> **Tipp**
>
> Ein Aktivsatz im Text kann zu einem Passivsatz bei den Aufgaben werden (oder umgekehrt):
>
> | bei den Aufgaben: | im Text: |
> |---|---|
> | **Passiv** | **Aktiv** |
> | 1B *They were removed from …* | *… children had to _____ their parents.* |

> **Tipp**
>
> Die Rolle von **Synonymen** (Wörter mit ähnlicher Bedeutung, wie *pretty – beautiful*) hast du oben in **1** schon gesehen. Bei *Multiple Choice*-Aufgaben spielen auch **Antonyme** (Wörter mit gegensätzlicher Bedeutung, wie *pretty – ugly*) oft eine Rolle.
> Dieses Wissen kann dir helfen, die richtige Lösung zu finden, z. B. hier:
> • Zu *die* und *disease* in Lösung A gibt es im Text keine Synonyme oder Antonyme.
>   Lösung A kannst du also wahrscheinlich ausschließen.
> • Zu *remove* und *parents* in Lösung B gibt es im Text Synonyme, nämlich _____ und _____.
>   Lösung B könnte also die richtige Lösung sein.
> • Zu *stay* in Lösung C gibt es im Text einen Gegensatz, nämlich _____.
>   Lösung C ist daher wahrscheinlich auch falsch.
> • Zu *wanted to (leave)* in Lösung D gibt es im Text auch einen Gegensatz, nämlich _____.
>   Lösung D ist daher wahrscheinlich auch falsch.

3 Fragen beantworten *(Answer the questions)*

- *Read paragraph 3 of Australia's Stolen Generations again.*
- *Then answer the questions.*

1 What did the Aboriginal children have to do in their new homes?

_____

_____

(2 points)

Tipp

Bei Fragen mit **zwei** Punkten musst du **zwei verschiedene** Antworten geben, um die volle Punktzahl zu bekommen.

Tipp

Die Satzstruktur der gestellten Frage kann dich dazu zwingen
- die **Informationen** aus dem Text **umzudrehen**:

im Text:	deine Antwort:
The children (...) were not allowed to speak their own language.	*They had to speak* _____.

- einen **Passivsatz** in einen **Aktivsatz** umzuwandeln (oder umgekehrt):

im Text:	deine Antwort:
... they were given the typical foods of white Australians ...	*They had to* _____ *the typical foods of white Australians.*

- *You cannot find the answer to the following question directly in the text:*

2 How did the Aboriginal children feel in their new homes?

_____ (2 points)

Tipp

Bei solchen Fragen musst du die Antwort aus dem Gegebenen schliessen. Stell dir vor, du wärst aus deiner Familie gerissen und in eine unbekannte Famlie gegeben worden mit unbekannter Sprache, unbekanntem Essen und unbekannter Wohnkultur. Wie würdest du dich fühlen?

4 Richtig/Falsch-Aufgaben *(True/False)*

- *Now read paragraph 4 of Australia's Stolen Generations.*
- *Decide whether the statement is true or false and tick (✓) the correct box.*

Tipp

Achte auf **Sammelbegriffe**, die stellvertretend für eine Reihe von Beispielen verwendet werden können:

im Text:	in der Aufgabe:
families, language, music, way of life	Sammelbegriff: _____

Außerdem gibt es hier eine **synonyme Formulierung**:

im Text:	in der Aufgabe:
... contact with their (...) was broken off	_____ _____

In time, Aboriginal Australians lost touch with their culture.

This statement is ...

☐ true   ☐ false

Also kann das *statement* nur _____ sein.

5 Zuordnungsaufgaben *(Matching)*

Bei dieser Leseverstehensaufgabe liest du fünf Personenbeschreibungen. Anschließend ordnest du diesen Personen sieben Texte zu (jeder Person zwei Texte, wobei meist einige Texte mehrfach zugeordnet werden können). Um dieses Aufgabenformat kennenzulernen und zu üben, geht es hier in der Training Section zunächst nur um drei Menschen und sechs Aktivitäten (A – F), wobei jede Person nur einer Aktivität zugeordnet werden muss.

Holiday activities

- *These young people (1–3) want to take part in a holiday activity.*
- *First read the information about the people, then look at the descriptions of the activities (A – F) on page 16 – 17.*
- *In each case find the activity each person would want to do. Write the letter of the activity in the box next to the person's name.*
- *Each activity can only be chosen once.*

No.	Activity	The people	
1			**Karen** loves discovering and exploring new places. Her financial resources are limited, so she is prepared to put up with fairly basic accommodation. She is more interested in spending time with like-minded people, as eager as she is to tackle new experiences and challenges.
2			**Jack** is a sports freak, and does well in everything from football to climbing, from kayaking to camping. He does well in both team and individual sports. But while he loves doing sport himself, his passion during the holidays is to share these skills with children from deprived areas of the country.
3			**Celina** is into arts and crafts of all kinds. She makes her own clothes, she restores and paints old furniture, and she has even done a course in colouring glass. Rather than doing more of a skill in which she is already well versed, however, she prefers to test herself against new challenges.

A

The Buxton Sports Academy offers holiday courses in a range of sports that include sailing, tennis, climbing, boxing and squash, as well as team sports such as football, rugby and hockey. Professional coaches who are used to working with young people give a thorough training and develop each individual's skills.

> **Tipp**
>
> Jack mag Sport – und doch ist **A** nicht die richtige Antwort. Er sucht etwas anderes. Siehst du, was?

B

Many families have old chairs or faded chests of drawers up in the attic or out in the garden shed – pieces of furniture that were once a source of pride and joy, and which could become so again. This 5-day residential course teaches students how to remove old paint and varnish, how to deal with stains and wood-worms, and how to bring colour back into faded wood. Suitable for beginners or experienced woodworkers.

> **Tipp**
>
> *Furniture* kommt bei Celina vor – und doch ist **B** nicht das passende Angebot für sie. Warum nicht?
> _____

C

Fancy a special adventure? Then join us on the expedition of a lifetime: a rail journey from London to Singapore!
We'll take the train to Moscow, then the Trans-Siberian Railway to Beijing (six nights on the train). After spending one night in Beijing, we'll continue via Hanoi and Ho Chi Minh City (formerly Saigon) in Vietnam, from where there are frequent bus connections via Phnom Penh to Bangkok in Thailand.
The final journey is a two-night trip to Singapore by train. Cost of the trip: £4999.

> **Tipp**
>
> Wow! Was für eine tolle Reise, und Karen mag Reisen. Und doch ist **C** nicht die richtige Antwort für sie. Warum nicht?
> _____

D

The Haxby Pottery Farm runs residential pottery courses for all ages and abilities. Create your own pots or sculptures, and make vases for your home or ceramic presents to give away. It's a great way to develop your pottery skills or learn a new craft, and make new friends. Phone Edna on 01826 34591 for more details.

> **Tipp**
>
> *Pots, vases, sculptures* ... kommen bei keinem der drei Teenager vor. Die Gesamtsituation ist aber wichtiger als Einzelwörter. Warum passt sie am besten zu Celina?
> _____

E

Every year we run a two-week residential camp in August in the heart of the Derbyshire Dales for inner-city children from the Greater Manchester area. The children have been selected by social workers working with families in some of the poorest inner-city wards, with the aim of giving the children new opportunities and their parents a break.
We always need volunteer assistants to help us run the courses: we cover board and lodging, but can offer no pay.

> **Tipp**
>
> Zu wem passt dieser Text – und warum?
> _____

F

Three intrepid hikers are looking for a fourth member to join them on a ten-day hike in the Italian Alps. Overnight stays in mountain huts and shelters, or in tents if necessary.
We have an old car to get us to Italy and kindly ask for a contribution to the cost of the fuel.

> **Tipp**
>
> Zu wem passt dieser Text – und warum?
> _____

3. Aufgaben zu längeren Texten

Filming in New Zealand

New Zealand's breathtaking landscape has long attracted the world's top film directors.

The *Lord of the Rings* trilogy, for example, was filmed in different areas of New Zealand, mainly, though not exclusively, in the country's national parks. The films made use of spectacular mountains such as Mount Ngauruhoe, a treeless live volcano, and of rivers, lakes and wild canyons. But scenes were also filmed in the softer and less dramatic looking green hills near Matamata.

One of the advantages of filming in New Zealand is that the population density is so low, with only four and half million people in a country more or less the same size as the United Kingdom (population: 64 million). So there are fewer buildings, roads and power lines to spoil the views of open countryside.

Disney's award-winning family movie *Pete's Dragon*, produced in 2015, also made use of New Zealand's landscape. The producer required giant redwood trees, a wild river where a bear could scare the hero, and bare mountains with cliffs from which a dragon could appear. All this was filmed in New Zealand, too. The wonderfully-named Whakarewarewa Forest near Rotorua has Californian redwood trees, the McLaren Falls Park features the wild river and the dramatic Deer Park Heights near Queenstown provided the remote and rugged mountains needed. And a helicopter company based in Queenstown helped to film the scene where the dragon flew over the mountains – not the only example of how filming brings employment to more than just actors and producers.

The Lord of the Rings – The Fellowship of the Ring
(New Line Cinema, USA/NZ 2001)

Indeed, many of the visual effects that make the dragon so lifelike were created in digital animation offices in Wellington, New Zealand's capital and second largest city – which has itself featured in a number of films. In the 2005 remake of the film classic *King Kong*, for example, many of the scenes supposedly set in New York were actually filmed in Wellington.

This means that the southernmost capital city in the world has a thriving film industry and professional experience of working with some leading film directors in the world.

Mount Ngauruhoe, New Zealand

6 Den Textteilen Überschriften zuordnen *(Match headings to the parts of the text)*

> • *Match the six correct headings to the parts of the text (1–6).*
> • *Be careful – there are two headings more than you need.*

A	A VARIETY OF LANDSCAPES
B	A LONG WAY FROM HOME
C	FILMING FROM THE AIR
D	FEW INHABITANTS
E	THE POWER OF NATURAL BEAUTY
F	KNOWHOW IS KING
G	ENGLISH MAKES IT EASY
H	NEW ZEALAND OR USA?

part of the text	1	2	3	4	5	6
heading						

7 Auswahlaufgaben *(Multiple choice)*

> • *Read these statements about the text on pp. 22/23.*
> • *Put a tick (✓) in the box next to the correct answer.*
> • *Only one answer is correct in each case.*

1 The *Lord of the Rings* trilogy was filmed ...

    A ☐ in various regions of New Zealand.

    B ☐ in national parks only.

    C ☐ in just one part of New Zealand.

    D ☐ on Mount Ngauruhoe only.

2 All the scenes of the *Lord of the Rings* were filmed ...

    A ☐ in wild hills near Matamata.

    B ☐ in spectacular and less spectacular scenery.

    C ☐ on a volcano famous for its trees.

    D ☐ in the most dramatic parts of the country.

3 New Zealand has …

A ☐ fewer people per square kilometre than the United Kingdom.

B ☐ about as many people per square kilometre as the United Kingdom.

C ☐ more people per square kilometre than the United Kingdom.

D ☐ about the same number of inhabitants as the United Kingdom.

4 Disney's movie *Pete's Dragon* …

A ☐ was partly filmed in the city of Wellington.

B ☐ gave work to a local company that flies helicopters.

C ☐ brought redwood trees from California to New Zealand.

D ☐ both B + C

5 Wellington …

A ☐ is New Zealand's biggest city.

B ☐ is further south than any other capital city.

C ☐ has good scenery, but no local film industry.

D ☐ all of them (A + B + C)

8 Zuordnungsaufgaben *(Matching)*

Work practice assignments

> • *Decide which of the work practice assignments described in the texts (A – H) is the most suitable for the teenagers below (1 – 5).*
> • *Write the correct letter in the box next to the picture.*

No.	Assignment	The teenagers	
1			Jonny has always been interested in things that grow. One of his favourite possessions is the microscope that his parents gave him for his last birthday because he loves analysing what leaves and flowers look like when magnified. But he's even happier when he can follow up his interest outdoors.
2			Samina started making things when she was only three years old. She began by sticking things together, then she went through a phase of knitting, and now she loves working creatively with wood, making both stand-alone works of art and practical objects for around the house.

3			Tadek speaks fluent Polish, German and English, but as though that is not enough he is also teaching himself Arabic and Japanese. "Languages are the key to meeting people," he says, "and there's nothing more fascinating in the world than people."
4			Katja loves making cakes, brownies and biscuits, and likes trying to make different sorts of bread. Not surprising that her favourite TV show is the Great British Bake-Off! Her most recent discovery is a sweet loaf traditionally made at Easter in the Ukraine.
5			Zoe is a friendly, tolerant person, but what makes her really angry is poor website design. She can't stand sites that look boring, are difficult to use or have information that is out of date. "There's no excuse for it," she says. "It's easy enough to produce an attractive web design – even quite a complicated one."

A

We welcome students to our friendly chemist's shop just off the market square. You will help serve customers and will have the opportunity to help us decorate the shop in the all-important lead-up to Christmas. In addition to medicines and cosmetics we also serve lunchtime sandwiches.

B

Tourists come to our city from all over the world, and many want to know more about our city's fascinating history. Here at *City Tours* we provide walking tours in an ever-growing number of different languages. Do your work experience here and you are sure to engage with interested clients from around the globe.

C

Horace's is the largest Garden Centre in town, with the widest choice of trees, shrubs and plants. We are happy to train students who share our passion for everything that grows in the garden. In addition to working at the till, you will learn how to breed plants from seeds and how to pack plants safely for orders by post.

D

K&J Logistics (formerly *Liptons Removals*) have been in the business of moving homes for over 100 years and enjoy an enviable reputation for reliability. We deal both with moves within our city and moves to countries abroad, and we have recently developed a new line in renting out vans. Your work experience will of course involve some carrying of furniture, but we'll also give you useful advice on looking after engines.

E

This is a young and innovative company, and in your work experience here you'll find yourself working with people not much older than yourself! Some will be working on new computer games, others will be developing apps for customers as varied as *United Biscuits* and *Featherstone Tyres*. What unites us is a passion for good quality digital work – and if you have good ideas in this field, we'll be happy to hear them!

F

Little People provides a safe, happy environment for pre-school children. We open at 7 am each workday and can look after your child for an hour or two, or all the way through till we close at 6 pm. All our assistants are qualified and of course we provide all children with snacks and meals.

G

I taught Technology for several years before setting up a new business as a freelance carpenter. My first orders were for chairs and window frames, but I have been able to branch out and tackle orders like shepherd's huts and church pews. I now have two full-time assistants, so in your work experience you will be in a team of four. I'll show you how to use a wide range of tools and help you to practise a range of skills. Welcome to the team!

H

We opened our shop three years ago, when Karen spotted the lack of a baker's shop in this part of town. Since then we have grown from success to success, with our fresh bakery products flying off the shelves. Come and join us for your work experience, and you'll pick up baking tips and tricks that will be useful to you for life.

9 Gemischte Aufgabenformate *(Mixed tasks)*

Indian food in Britain

Indian cooking has been popular in Britain for a long time. Britain's first Indian restaurant opened its doors in 1810, and in 1774 a British cookery book contained recipes for Indian dishes. Many British people were familiar with Indian food because Britain ruled large parts of India, and British soldiers, administrators, engineers and their families spent many years of their lives in India. They grew to like Indian food and wanted more of it when they returned to Britain.

It wasn't easy, back then, to get hold of fresh Indian spices. If they were imported from India, they could spend up to six months in transport by sea, by which time they had often lost their flavour. So people experimented with herbs and spices from the Mediterranean or from Latin America, and slowly the 'Indian' dishes in Britain began to differ from the originals in India.

What was easy to buy in Britain was a yellow powder called *curry powder*, which is a mix of dried herbs and spices. And the many individual flavourful dishes served in India came to be replaced by one standard dish called *curry*. In India, in contrast, you can't buy *curry*. It would be as absurd as asking for a soup in Europe without saying what sort of soup you want.

In the early 20th century, immigration from India increased. Many immigrants were seamen who worked on British ships and decided to stay in Britain when their ships returned to India. Some of them opened small restaurants. They were often from countries now known as Bangladesh and Pakistan, which, back then, were all part of British India, so their food was called Indian food. India became an independent country in 1948, and Pakistan and Bangladesh later split off from India to become independent countries too. Today, well over half of all Indian restaurants in Britain have Bangladeshi owners and workers – but they are usually still called Indian.

The cafe owners soon realized that nobody in Britain was selling hot food late at night. They realized that people walking home after a drink in the pub or from a late shift at work were only too happy to buy hot food. These customers did not have time to sit down and eat; they wanted their food in a form that they could carry home. This was the birth of the Indian takeaway.

For years, *chicken tikka masala* was the most popular dish served in Indian takeaways. But a recent trend is that customers are becoming more adventurous and trying out a wider range of dishes. This is partly due to the influence of TV food programmes and comments on social media: customers are now more informed about the range of food available. It also reflects people's concerns about their own health, with many customers looking for lower-calory dishes.

> - *First read the text.*
> - *Then do the tasks (1–6).*
> - *For tasks 1 and 3 tick (✓) the correct box.*
> - *For tasks 2 and 4 complete the sentences.*
> - *For tasks 5 and 6 decide if the statements are true or false and tick (✓) the correct box.*

1 A British book from 1774 …

    A ☐ warned its readers against eating Indian food.

    B ☐ told its readers how to prepare Indian food.

    C ☐ explained how to open an Indian restaurant.

2 Many British people liked Indian food in Britain 200 years ago because …

_____

3 Herbs and spices that were imported from India …

    A ☐ were often too expensive.

    B ☐ often did not have much taste.

    C ☐ were too spicy for people in Britain.

4 You can't buy *curry* in India because …

_____

5 Indian restaurants are often not really Indian.

    This statement is … ☐ true ☐ false

6 People are now increasingly buying the same food in Indian takeaways.

    This statement is … ☐ true ☐ false

> - *You cannot find the answer to the following question directly in the text:*

7 Most Indian restaurants in Britain have Bangladeshi owners and workers.
Why do you think the restaurants are usually still called 'Indian' restaurants?

Sprachgebrauch – *Use of language*

1. Ablauf und Bewertung der Abschlussarbeit

Ablauf

Use of Language besteht aus zwei Teilen:
- *Mediation*
- *Words and structures*.

Bei *Mediation* vermittelst du für einen deutschsprachigen Sprecher, der einen englischen Text verstehen muss. Du sollst den Text nicht Wort für Wort übersetzen, sondern das Wichtige in deinen eigenen Worten übertragen.
Danach liest du einen deutschen Text und gibst die wichtigsten Punkte auf Englisch wieder.

Du brauchst keine Angst vor Grammatik- oder Rechtschreibfehlern in deinen Antworten zu haben. Solange man versteht, was du geschrieben hast, gehen sie in diesem Prüfungsteil nicht in die Bewertung ein. Bei *Mediation* wird jede Lösung akzeptiert, durch die der Empfänger die Mitteilung versteht und darauf angemessen reagieren kann.

Bei *Word and structures* bearbeitest du einen oder zwei Texte. Die Texte haben Lücken, und du musst die Lücken füllen: du wählst zum Beispiel das richtige Wort aus einer Liste von möglichen Wörtern, oder du schreibst die richtige Form von einem gegebenen Verb.

In diesem Teil der Abschlussarbeit geht es um Genauigkeit, und bei Grammatik- oder Rechtschreibfehlern werden Punkte abgezogen.

Bewertung

Mediation und *Words and structures* machen <u>zusammen</u> 25 % der Note der Abschlussarbeit aus.

2. Mediation: Typische Aufgabenformate in Hessen

In diesem Kapitel lernst du die typischen Aufgabenformate kennen, die dich bei der Abschlussarbeit im Bereich *Mediation* erwarten.

Die blauen Tipp-Kästen enthalten nützliche Strategien, wie du mit häufigen Schwierigkeiten umgehen kannst.

1 *Mediation* vom Englischen ins Deutsche

Du liest einen Text auf Englisch und vermittelst für eine deutschsprachige Person, die Englisch nicht gut versteht. Dabei suchst du zuerst das Hauptthema oder der Kernpunkt des Textes, und dann wählst du vier weitere Informationen, die von Interesse sein könnten. Das heißt natürlich, dass du manche Informationen im Text ignorierst, weil sie nicht zu den interessantesten zählen.

Deine Kollegin Aylin interessiert sich für Motorräder und hat im Internet diese Infos zu einem besonders spannenden Motorradrennen gefunden.

The TT race – the most exciting motorbike race in the world!

The Isle of Man is a small island between Britain and Ireland. It is famous for its motorcycle racing.

This text is from a blog written by a resident on the Isle of Man.

I live on one of Europe's quietest islands – the Isle of Man, a small island in the Irish Sea about halfway between England and Ireland. We have beautiful unspoilt countryside with
5　narrow country roads. The roads are usually wonderfully quiet, but all this changes when the TT motorbike races take place.

The TT (or Tourist Trophy, to give it its official name) is one of the most famous motorcycle
10　racing events in the world, and the amazing thing is that it doesn't take place on a special racing track, but on public roads. The riders, who have all had to bring their bikes over to the island by ferry, set off individually in ten-second
15　intervals and race against the clock. In other words, their aim is not only to overtake the riders in front of them, but to be the fastest rider overall.

The TT was started in 1907. Back then the
20　race used the shorter St John's course, which was 15 miles long. The course was extended in 1911 and is now 37¾ miles (about 50 km) long. And that is just one lap! The top racers in the

Superbike class cover six laps, averaging close to 130 mph (that about 210 km/hour).

They only stop to refuel and change wheels. If that sounds dangerous, it is. 246 people lost　25 their lives during the event between 1907 and 2015 – 141 competitors and 105 spectators and other members of the public. Some safety features were brought in after a number of riders boycotted the event in the early 1970s, the　30 race remains as exciting as ever.

Although it is called the TT race, the event consists of a number of races, with different categories of bikes: Superbike, Senior, Superstock, Supersport, Lightweight, etc. The event　35 always takes place over a two week period at the end of May and beginning of June. The public roads used by the racers are closed to the public for a week of practice runs followed by a week of racing.　40

1　Aylin bittet dich, ihr zu erklären, um was es in diesen Infos geht. Nenne auf Deutsch das Hauptthema (vollständige Sätze sind nicht notwendig):

_____

Tipp

Du weißt schon, es geht hier um ein Motorradrennen. Das brauchst du nicht wiederholen. Aber was könnte einen Motorradfan interessieren: Wann das erste Rennen stattfand? Wohl nicht. Wo das Rennen zu sehen ist? In welcher Hinsicht es anders ist, als alle andere Rennen? Wohl eher.

2　Nenne vier weitere wichtige Informationen zu diesem Motorradrennen auf Deutsch (vollständige Sätze sind nicht notwendig):

Tipp

Lies den Text sorgfältig durch und markiere die Stellen mit Infos, die Aylin interessieren könnten. Wähle dann die vier interessantesten Infos.

A　_____

B　_____

C　_____

D　_____

2 *Mediation* **vom Deutschen ins Englische**

Fußballturnier

Du sollst einen Text auf Deutsch lesen. Eine englischsprachige Person stellt ein paar Fragen zum Text, und du sollst die Informationen auf Englisch wiedergeben. Außerdem sollst du Informationen aussuchen, die für die andere Person von Interesse sein könnten.

Neues Turnier mit gemischten Mannschaften

Die Fußballklubs unserer Region haben eine lange Tradition, fürchten sich aber nicht vor neuen Entwicklungen. Dazu gehört die Erfahrung in immer mehr Sportvereinen, dass Jungen und Mädchen davon profitieren, wenn sie die Gelegenheit haben, nach Altersklassen zusammen zu trainieren und zu spielen.

Aus diesem Grunde hat sich die Stadt für ein Turnier mit gemischten Jungen- und Mädchen-Mannschaften entschieden. Es werden im ersten Jahr drei Altersgruppen zugelassen:

– Gruppe A: Mannschaften von 11- und 12-jährigen,
– Gruppe B: Mannschaften von 13- und 14-jährigen,
– Gruppe C: Mannschaften von 15- und 16-jährigen.

Die Spiele der ersten Runde des Turniers finden im September nächsten Jahres statt. Meldeschluss für die Mannschaften ist Ende Mai. Die nähere Organisation des Turniers ist davon abhängig, wie viele Mannschaften sich für das Turnier melden. Details dazu wird es bis Ende Juli geben. Wir hoffen, dass ältere Spieler sowohl beim Training der Jüngeren als auch bei der Organisation des Turniers helfen werden.

Nach ersten Kontakten mit den Fußballklubs in unserer Region rechnet die Stadt mit einem großen Zulauf an Interessenten. Das gilt sowohl für Teilnehmer als auch für Zuschauer. Es ist unsere Hoffnung, dass das neue Turnier zu einer jährlichen Institution wird, und dass der Rahmen sich über die nächsten Jahre erweitert, sodass auch ältere Spieler und Spielerinnen zukünftig teilnehmen können.

Mannschaften werden nur dann zugelassen, wenn sie aus mindestens vier Jungen und mindestens vier Mädchen bestehen.

Die Teilnahmegebühr beträgt € 20,00 pro Mannschaft.
Es wird für dieses erste Turnier spezielle T-Shirts und Erinnerungsmedaillen geben.

1 Im Fußballklub lernst du ein neues Mitglied des Klubs kennen, Adelola, ein 16-jähriges Mädchen aus Nigeria. Sie möchte gerne in einer Meisterschaft spielen und fragt dich, worum es in dieser Mitteilung geht.
Notiere dir zunächst auf Englisch die Hauptinformation der Mitteilung (vollständige Sätze sind nicht notwendig):

> **Tipp**
>
> Was ist entscheidend in diesem Turnier?
> In welcher Hinsicht ist es anders als die meisten?
> Schon der Titel weist darauf hin!

2 Notiere auf Englisch fünf weitere wichtige Informationen, die Adelola interessieren könnten (vollständige Sätze sind nicht notwendig):

A _____

B _____

C _____

D _____

E _____

> **Tipp**
>
> Um zu entscheiden, was Adelola interessieren könnte: Versuche die Sache mit ihren Augen zu sehen und frag dich, was sie interessieren könnte.
> Du hast z.B. erfahren, dass sie 16 Jahre alt ist – gibt es da Chancen, dass sie in diesem Turnier spielen könnte?
>
> Hab keine Angst, manche Infos als unwichtig beiseite zu lassen. Adelola möchte z.B. im Turnier spielen – dass der Klub Mitglieder sucht, um bei der Organisation zu helfen, ist für Adelola nicht so relevant.

3. Words and structures: Typische Aufgabenformate in Hessen

In diesem Kapitel lernst du die typischen Aufgabenformate kennen, die dich bei der Abschlussarbeit im Bereich **Words and structures** erwarten.

Die blauen Tipp-Kästen enthalten nützliche Strategien, wie du mit häufigen Schwierigkeiten umgehen kannst.

1 Lückentext mit Wortspeicher *(Banked gap-filling)*

- *Read the text, then choose the correct words from the box to fill in the gaps.*
- *Use each word once only.*
- *There are more words than you need.*
- *Be careful – one gap is at the beginning of the sentence.*

but • came • come • didn't • do • doesn't • don't • from • get • he • of • once • one • that • to • too • two • who

Ian Watson lives in Chilham, a village

not far (1) _____ Canterbury.

Tipp

1 Lies immer den ganzen Satz. Das hilft dir zu sehen, was für ein Wort fehlt. In (1) kann z. B. kein Verb vorkommen – somit fallen *came, come, get* usw aus. *Not far from* und *not far to* sind beide möglich – aber dem Sinn nach passt hier nur eins von beiden.

Every morning he waits for

a bus (2) _____ takes

him to school in Canterbury.

Tipp

2 Hier fehlt ein Wort, das zwei ganze Satzteile verbindet, z.B. *that* oder *who*. Wie kannst du zwischen den beiden unterscheiden?

But Ian (3) _____ like taking

the bus. It's often late and more than

(4) _____ he has had to phone

his parents and ask them to (5) _____

and fetch him by car. Ian is a keen cyclist.

Tipp

3 Hier fehlt ein Verb. Bei Verben stelle dir immer drei Fragen:
- Positiv oder negativ?   Hier: *negativ* _____
- Present, Past, Future?   Hier: _____
- Singular oder Plural?   Hier: _____

(6) _____ would prefer to cycle

to school, but his parents say that the road

is (7) _____ dangerous.

Tipp

6 Das erste Wort des Satzes fehlt. Vergiss nicht die Großschreibung des ersten Buchstabens.

2 Auswahlaufgaben *(Multiple choice)*

Gender equality

> • *Read the text, then tick (✓) the correct words.*

1 These days we have more …

- A ☐ informed
- B ☐ inform
- C ☐ information
- D ☐ informing

about gender equality than ever before.

Tipp

Verstehst du *gender equality* nicht? Keine Panik! Du kannst trotzdem alle Aufgaben lösen.

Tipp

1 Was folgt auf *we have more* …? *We have more cats, pens, CDs,* … Das sind alles Substantive – keine Verben. Also brauchst du hier ein Substantiv mit *INFORM*…

2 And most people …

- A ☐ agree
- B ☐ agrees
- C ☐ agreed
- D ☐ agreeing

that gender equality a good thing.

Tipp

2 Hier brauchst du ein Verb. Stelle dir immer die drei Fragen, die du schon in Aufgabe 1 gesehen hast:
Positiv oder negativ?
Present, Past, Future?
Singular oder Plural?

3 These days girls often perform …

- A ☐ well
- B ☐ good
- C ☐ better
- D ☐ best

than boys at school.

Tipp

3 Adjektiv + than = Komparativ
z. B. *(BIG) than = bigger than*
Good ist aber unregelmäßig → …?… *than*

4 And yet …

- A ☐ is
- B ☐ are
- C ☐ there is
- D ☐ there are

still too few women in top jobs. Why is this?

Tipp

4 Es gibt auf Englisch
 there … (Singular)
oder *there* … (Plural).
Wie weißt du, ob du hier Singular oder Plural brauchst?

3 Bildung von Verben *(Verb formation)*

> • *Complete the text with the correct form of the verbs.*

Hi Emma, I was sorry (**1 hear**) _____ that you

haven't been well.

I hope very much that you (**2 feel**) _____

better now.

Do you think you (**3 be able to**) _____

come bowling tomorrow?

If you like, I (**4 come**) _____ to your house

and we can (**5 catch**) _____ the bus together.

I (**6 never be**) _____ bowling before, so I'm

really looking forward to it! All the best, Tim

Tipp
1 *sorry + to + Verb*

Tipp
2 Welche Zeitform bei Signalwort: *now?*

Tipp
3 Welche Zeitform bei Signalwort: *tomorrow?*

Tipp
4 *If*-Satz!

Tipp
5 *can + Verb (ohne to)*

Tipp
6 *ever/never + be → present perfect!*

Schreiben – *Text production*

1. Ablauf und Bewertung der Abschlussarbeit

Ablauf bei der Text production

Dieser Teil der Prüfung besteht aus zwei Aufgaben und du musst dich für die eine oder die andere Aufgabe entscheiden. Zum Beispiel:
– Du siehst ein lustiges Foto und stellst dir vor, wie es zu dem Foto gekommen ist.
– Du liest und beantwortest eine Mail oder einen Brief.
– Du schreibst Pro- und Kontra-Argumente zu einem gegebenen Thema.

In beiden Aufgaben musst du 150 Wörter schreiben.

Ein zweisprachiges Wörterbuch ist erlaubt. Elektronische Wörterbücher dürfen aber nicht verwendet werden.

Bewertung bei der Text production

Das Schreiben macht 25% der Note der Abschlussarbeit aus.
Punkte werden für **Inhalt** und **Sprache** vergeben.
Folgende Kriterien tragen zu deiner Note bei:

- **Inhalt:** Es gibt Punkte dafür, dass du …
    - die Aufgabe vollständig löst,
    - alle Aspekte eindeutig, detailliert und differenziert darstellst,
    - nur wenige Wiederholungen und Abschweifungen hast,
    - deinen Text kohärent (= zusammenhängend) und logisch gliederst.

- **Sprache:** Es gibt Punkte dafür, dass …
    - das Lesen deines Textes keine Mühe bereitet,
    - es sich um einen sehr klar formulierten Text handelt,
    - du komplexe Sätze bildest (mit Haupt- und Nebensätzen, *time phrases* etc.)
    - dein Text durch Verwendung von Bindewörtern (Konnektoren) logisch aufgebaut ist,
    - du einen vielseitigen und zutreffenden Wortschatz und idiomatische Wendungen benutzt,
    - du die Wörter richtig schreibst,
    - du verschiedene grammatische Strukturen sicher verwendest,
    - man versteht, was du sagen willst, auch wenn bei komplizierten Sätzen vereinzelte Wortschatz- oder Grammatikfehler vorkommen.

2. Typische Aufgabenformate in Hessen

Im Folgenden lernst du beispielhafte Aufgabenformate kennen, die dich bei der Abschlussprüfung im Bereich Schreiben erwarten können. Die blauen Kästen enthalten nützliche Hinweise und Hilfen.

1 The story behind the picture

a) Arbeitsanweisung:

Lies dir die Arbeitsanweisung und den Tipp genau durch.

> *What is the story behind the picture? Write a text and*
> *include at least four of the following aspects:*
> - *Where is it?*
> - *Who is this person?*
> - *Why is she making a funny face for this photo?*
> - *What is she thinking?*
> - *What will happen next?*

Tipp

Um alle Punkte zu bekommen, musst du mindestens vier Fragen beantworten. Markiere also die Fragen, die du beantworten möchtest. So verlierst du keine Punkte, weil du versehentlich eine Frage übersehen hast.

b) Sprache:

Du bekommst Punkte für deine **klare sprachliche Darstellung.** Es geht also darum, so wenige Fehler wie möglich zu machen.

Wie könnte deine Lösung aussehen? Hier ist ein Beispiel.

Aber Achtung:

- Es ist zu kurz (nur 105 Wörter).
- Die blau markierten Wörter sind fehlerhaft.

Lies die Hinweise in den Kästen und verbessere die Fehler.

1 Rechtschreibung!	**2** Falsches Pronomen. *His* ist männlich.
3 *present tense*: die 3. Person von Verben endet auf ...?	**4** Groß- oder Kleinschreibung?
5 Falsche Verneinung!	
6 Falsche Zeitform des Verbs. Hier brauchst du *simple past*.	**7** Falsche Frageform! *Do you ...?*
	8 Rechtschreibung!

I thing[1] this girl looks really funny! His[2] name is Sheila, and she is a model for an agency that make[3] adverts for cosmetics. So she spends all day in front of the Camera[4]. She always has to smile. She not looks[5] normal. And that gets on her nerves.

So yesterday evening, after six hours of photos and filming, she put a flower in her mouth and make[6] a funny face.

A photographer saw her and took a photo. And know you[7] what? I think the photo will be a great success in an advert, because it is funnyer[8] and more original than most photos.

> **Tipp**
>
> Schau dir noch einmal deine letzten drei Klassenarbeiten an. Erstelle eine Checkliste mit acht bis zehn Fehlern, die mehrmals aufgetaucht sind. Beispiel:
>
> *wrong:*   *right:*
>
> I ~~not like~~ this.   →   I <u>don't like</u> this.
>
> Sieh dir diese Liste immer wieder an, um diese Fehler in Zukunft zu vermeiden.

c) Dein Text:
Nun schreibe deinen eigenen Text zum Foto.
Schau dir dafür noch einmal die Arbeitsanweisungen in **a)** an. Schreibe 150 Wörter.

d) Überprüfe deinen Text auf mögliche Fehler.
Nimm dir am Ende der Prüfung Zeit, deine Texte noch einmal zu überprüfen. Wir machen alle Fehler beim Schreiben. Jede Korrektur, die du hier machen kannst, bringt dir Punkte.

Inhalt	Sprache
Hast du mindestens vier Fragen beantwortet: – Wo wurde das Foto gemacht? – Wer ist die Person? – Um was für eine Situation handelt es sich? – Was denkt die Person? / Was könnte als Nächstes passieren? Hast du ca. 150 Wörter geschrieben?	Stimmen die Zeitformen der Verben? Sind alle Wörter richtig geschrieben? Hast du auf Groß- und Kleinschreibung geachtet? Hast du irgendwo ein falsches Wort verwendet? Stimmen der Satzbau und die Verneinungen?

e) Jetzt bist du Prüferin oder Prüfer ☺!
Du kannst bis 25 Punkte vergeben.

Bis zu …	Kriterien	Punkte
10 Punkte: Inhalt	Mindestens vier Fragen in den Anweisungen wurden voll und mit 140 bis 160 Wörtern beantwortet.	_____
5 Punkte: Organisation	Der Text ist klar und kohärent.	_____
5 Punkte: Grammatik	Die Grammtik ist größtenteils richtig. Grammatische Strukturen (z.B. Zeiten, Passiv, modale Verben, Vergleiche, adverbiale Strukturen, Adverbien) werden verwendet.	_____
5 Punkte: Wortschatz	Breiter Wortschatz, weitgehend fehlerfrei.	_____
	Gesamtpunkte	_____

Punkte: _____

Begründung: _____

▶ Fortsetzung (Seite 37) nach den Lösungen

Englisch

ABSCHLUSS-PRÜFUNGS-TRAINER

Hessen

Lösungen

Cornelsen

TRAINING SECTION: Hörverstehen ▶ S. 8–14

Calgary's skyways

1 Auswahlaufgaben (Multiple choice)
An underground city … C allows people to avoid the cold weather.

2 Zuordnungsaufgaben (Matching)
1 Burlington: **D** · *2 Stoney Creek:* **B** · *3 Kissimmee:* **A** · *4 Jacksonville:* **F** · *5 Jasper National Park:* **E**

3 Einsetzaufgaben (Fill in the gap)
1 overhead · *2 downtown/central*

4 Kurzantwort-Aufgaben (Give short answers)
1 **A** *They don't have to walk in the rain and cold. / are protected from the rain and cold. / are protected from the weather. / …*
B *They don't have to cross the roads. / are safe from the traffic. / are safer because they never have to cross a road. / …*
2 Because there is less life in the streets. / less life at street level. / Because the streets feel deserted. / are empty. / …

5 Richtig/Falsch-Aufgaben (True/False)
1 false · *2 true* · *3 true*

The Niagara Falls

1 **C** *are for the most part in Canada.*
2 They wear clothes/coats/ponchos against the rain. / They wear waterproof ponchos/raincoats/…
3 **B** *was the first state park in the USA.*
4 raise money
5 **B** *injured.*
6 **A** *mainly* · **B** *waterproof ponchos* · **C** *the country's oldest* · **D** *raise money* · **E** *did hurt her head*

The Tour de Yorkshire

Auswahlaufgaben (Multiple choice)
1 **C** *began in Yorkshire.*
2 **C** *there were old yellow bicycles on the sides of the roads used by the race.*
3 **B** *did not expect the enthusiastic reaction from people in Yorkshire.*
4 **B** *left people in Yorkshire wanting to see more cycling races.*
5 **A** *includes hills that are difficult even for experienced cyclists.*

Bob Marley

Richtig/Falsch-Aufgaben (True/False)
1 true · *2 true* · *3 false* · *4 false* · *5 true* · *6 true* · *7 false* · *8 false*

Top of the Rock

Notizen anfertigen (Note-taking)
B Central Park
C 8 am
D No waiting time / No queue
E 34 dollars
F can visit twice in one day / on the same day
G wear warm clothes

TRAINING SECTION: Leseverstehen ▶ S. 15–26

Australia's Stolen Generations

1 Den Textteilen Überschriften zuordnen (Find the correct headings)
1 **B** · *2* **D** · *3* **A** · *4* **E**

2 Auswahlaufgaben (Multiple choice)
What happened to thousands of Aboriginal children?
B *They were removed from their parents.*

3 Fragen beantworten (Answer the questions)
1 What did the Aboriginal children have to do in their new homes?
They had to speak English.
And they had to eat the typical foods of white Australians / eat foods that they weren't used to.

2 How did the Aboriginal children feel in their new homes?
They felt sad/homesick/worried/frightened/unsettled/etc.

4 Richtig/Falsch-Aufgaben (True/False)
true

Holiday activities

5 Zuordnungsaufgaben (Matching)
1 **F** · *2* **E** · *3* **D**
Tipp zu A: Jack möchte mit Kindern arbeiten.
Tipp zu B: Celina sucht ein neues Betätigungsfeld.
Tipp zu C: Diese Reise ist teuer, aber Karen hat nicht viel Geld.
Tipp zu D: Celina möchte etwas Neues ausprobieren.
Tipp zu E: Zu Jack, denn August ist Ferienzeit, und er möchte die Ferien mit Kindern verbringen.
Tipp zu F: Zu Karen, denn sie möchte mit Gleichgesinnten preiswert reisen.

Filming in New Zealand

6 Den Textteilen Überschriften zuordnen (Match headings to the parts of the text):
1 **E** · *2* **A** · *3* **D** · *4* **C** · *5* **H** · *6* **F**

7 Auswahlaufgaben (Multiple choice)
1 **A** *in various regions of New Zealand.*
2 **B** *in spectacular and less spectacular scenery.*
3 **A** *fewer people per square kilometre than the United Kingdom.*
4 **B** *gave work to a local company that flies helicopters.*
5 **B** *is further south than any other capital city.*

Work practice assignments

8 Zuordnungsaufgaben (Matching)
1 **C** · *2* **G** · *3* **B** · *4* **H** · *5* **E**

Indian food in Britain

9 Gemischte Aufgabenformate (Mixed tasks)
1 **B** *told its readers how to prepare Indian food.*
2 they had lived in India for a long time. / had spent many years of their lives in India. / …
3 **B** *often did not have much taste.*
4 there are many different types of curry. / the word "curry" is too general. / not specific enough. / …
5 true
6 false
7 British people don't know the workers are from Bangladesh/can't recognise whether the workers are from India or Bangladesh / the difference isn't important to them / force of habit

TRAINING SECTION: Sprachgebrauch ▶ S. 27–33

1 *Mediation* vom Englischen ins Deutsche
The TT race – the most exciting motorbike race in the world!
1 (Motorradrennen) auf der Isle of Man / auf öffentlichen Straßen

2 vier wichtige Informationen, z.B.:
A zwei Wochen Ende Mai/Anfang Juni
B eine Runde ist 50 km lang
C die Rennfahrer/innen können bis zu 6 Runden fahren
D es sind schon Menschen bei dem Rennen ums Leben gekommen

2 *Mediation* vom Deutschen ins Englische
Fußballturnier
1 competition is for boys and girls / mixed teams

2 fünf wichtige Informationen, z.B.:
A group C is for 16-year-olds
B first round in September next year
C teams must register before the end of May
D each team must have at least 4 boys and 4 girls
E each team must pay a 20 euro fee

Words and structures

1 Lückentext mit Wortspeicher *(Banked gap-filling)*
1 from
2 that/which
3 doesn't **Tipp:** *(negativ), present, Singular*
4 once
5 come
6 He
7 too

Gender equality
2 Auswahlaufgaben *(Multiple choice)*
1 C information
2 A agree
3 C better
4 D there are

3 Verb formation
1 to hear
2 are feeling
3 'll be able to / will be able to
4 'll come / will come
5 catch
6 've never been / have never been

TRAINING SECTION: Text production ▶ S. 33–41

2 Answer an email
Blau markiert sind Stellen, die den Inhalt der Aufgabe erfüllen. Grau markiert sind Konjunktionen, die Nebensätze einleiten.

> Hi Josh,
> Nice to hear from you.
>
> I had a great weekend, thanks, because I went camping in the mountains with my friend Sam. Dave had wanted to come too, but he didn't have time.
>
> We hiked along muddy valleys, we climbed steep hills and in the evening we cooked on an open fire. Although the weather was awful, it was great fun. The wet nights weren't great, but it was a great feeling when I stood on the the highest mountain that I had ever climbed!
>
> It would be great to see you here again! When are your next holidays?
>
> Best wishes, …

Verben im *simple past*:
had, went, didn't have, hiked, climbed, cooked, was (3x), weren't, stood (7 verschiedene)

Adjektive:
nice, great (5x), muddy, steep, open, awful, wet, highest, next, best (10 verschiedene)

Linking words (Konnektoren)
because, but (2x), and, although, when, that (6 verschiedene)

My weekend job
3 A summary

b) Beispiel 1
Sarah *is a student at school* and she usually *gets on well with* her parents. But now she has a weekend job *because* she needs money for her clothes, her phone and for going out with her friends. She works in a clothes shop on a Saturday or Sunday, and she works hard *although* it means she has to get up early. She *arrives on time,* she helps to prepare the shop and she helps the customers.
Sometimes she works at the till.
Her boss has said that she *is a good worker.* But Sarah's parents *are unhappy with her job and want her to give it up. They say that the job is bad for Sarah's health and for her progress at school. So now Sarah is in trouble with her parents.*

c) Beispiel 2
Sarah really *likes/loves/appreciates/…* her job. She's grateful for the opportunity to prove that she can work well in the adult world. And of course she's happy to earn some money because she *doesn't like asking* her parents for money.
But Sarah's parents aren't happy / don't think it's good / are disappointed that she has taken a job. They don't like the sort of clothes that she sells and say that she should work in a different kind of shop. And they're worried about her health and fear that she'll get behind with her school work and homework.
Sarah thinks that her parents' reaction is unfair. she didn't choose

to work in this shop – it was the only job she could get. She also thinks they're illogical: after all, the effect on her school work would be the same if she worked in a fair-trade shop. And finally, Sarah thinks that her parents' reaction doesn't really have anything to do with her job: they're unhappy, she says, because they worry that she will become too independent if she earns her own money.

Musterprüfung 1: Listening Comprehension ▶ S. 44 – 46

Part 1
A tour guide: Bo-Kaap
1 A *at the end of the 18th century.*
2 C *were Europeans.*
3 A *to work in South Africa.*
4 B *are Asian.*

A special plane
1 A *two European countries.*
2 C *twice as fast as the speed of sound.*
3 C *two hours and fifty-three minutes.*
4 B *it did not sell well.*

Part 2
Adverts
Advert 1: *Katy*
Advert 2: *Grace*
Advert 3: *Sam*
Advert 4: *Liz*
Advert 5: *Wayne*
Advert 6: *Livvy*
Advert 7: *Anna*

Part 3
A presentation about William Shakespeare
1 *wrote poems and plays / wrote 38 plays / his plays are performed today / his plays are performed in many countries*
2 *1564*
3 *John and Mary*
4 *18*
5 *died at age 11 / died young*
6 *London*
7 *(the) house where he was born*
8 *Shakespeare's classroom / where Shakespeare was a student*
9 *the old theatre / the theatre of Shakespeare's age*
10 *you stand / you are near the actors / tickets cheaper than other theatres*

Musterprüfung 1: Reading Comprehension ▶ S. 47 – 52

Good health in Australia?
1 E · 2 D · 3 A · 4 B · 5 F

High-rise living in Britain
1 C *were for poor families.*
2 A *taken down their 1960s tower blocks*
3 B *safe because burglars cannot break in so easily.*
4 C *they are easier to take care of.*
5 B *better quality than those built in the 1960s.*
6 D *don't need to worry about cleaning the communal areas.*
7 A *are often cheaper than other flats.*
8 C *like to see their children when they are playing.*
9 D *living in a house is better for you.*
10 A *helps against heart disease.*

My first journey abroad
1 *He was afraid of speaking a different language.*
2 *Philip persuaded him / he didn't want Philip to be alone.*
3 *They worked in a café.*
4 *A bedroom in a hostel.*
5 *He was called Philip/Filip, like Paul's friend.*
6 *He spoke / used words.*
 He drew.
 He acted / used his hands.
7 *They cheered. / They ate together.*
8 *He felt scared / frightened / nervous.*
9 *A crown.*

Musterprüfung 1: Use of language ▶ S. 53 – 55

Mediation
a) 1 *ob Carola Lucy helfen kann, in Deutschland einen Job zu finden*
   2 A *am liebsten einen Job im Theater*
     B *nicht nur im Bereich Schauspiel, sondern auch Ton, Beleuchtung oder Kostüme*
     C *ein paar Wochen Arbeit im Herbst*
     D *muss nicht bezahlt sein*

b) 1 *This theatre needs people to do different jobs (sound, lighting, front of house, etc).*
   2 A *can work for two weeks*
     B *workers must be over 15*
     C *includes evening and weekend work*
     D *max 35 hours a week*
     E *unpaid (but free theatre tickets)*

Words and structures
The Everglades
1 *south*
2 *their*
3 *which*
4 *how*
5 *huge*
6 *polluted*
7 *inhabitants*
8 *drying*
9 *replaced*
10 *quickly*
11 *worse*
12 *completed*
13 *from*
14 *pass*

Musterprüfung 1: Text production ▶ S. 56

Wegen der möglichen Bandbreite an unterschiedlichen Lösungen bei den längeren Schreibaufgaben (150 Wörter) werden für diese Teilaufgaben nur die inhaltlichen Aspekte knapp auf Deutsch skizziert. Siehe ausführlich dazu auch die Hinweise zur Bewertung von Inhalt und Sprache auf S. 36. Generell gilt, dass die folgenden Aspekte in deinem Text berücksichtigt sein sollten, um die volle Punktzahl zu bekommen:

- Du machst wenige Wiederholungen und schweifst nicht vom Thema ab.
- Dein Text lässt sich leicht lesen.
- Dein Text ist klar formuliert und logisch aufgebaut. Du verwendest Bindewörter (Konnektoren) wie *because*, *but*, *so* etc.
- Du verwendest einen vielseitigen Wortschatz und idiomatische Wendungen, z.B. *make a difference*.
- Du bist sicher in der Verwendung verschiedener grammatischer Strukturen.
- Auch wenn bei komplizierten Sätzen vereinzelte Wortschatz- oder Grammatikfehler vorkommen, versteht man, was du sagen willst.

Tipp: Zeig deinen Text doch einem Mitschüler oder einer Mitschülerin und lasse ihn oder sie beurteilen, ob du diese Aspekte berücksichtigt hast. Oder sprich deinen Lehrer oder deine Lehrerin an – sie können es am allerbesten beurteilen.

Musterprüfung 2: Listening Comprehension ▶ S. 57 – 59

Part 1
A report about St Kilda
1 *160 kilometres / 100 miles*
2 *birds*
3 *they were brought to Scotland*
4 *in a tent / on a campsite*

A report about Wales
1 C *not like English at all.*
2 A *speak a language like the Welsh language.*
3 B *a minority language in Wales.*
4 C *the north and west of Wales.*

Part 2
Radio notices
Notice 1: *Don't spread disease*
Notice 2: *Dispose of your rubbish responsibly*
Notice 3: *A new system*
Notice 4: *Safe toys?*
Notice 5: *Think of your weight*

Part 3
First job
1 *part-time work / weekend work*
2 A *Tom has never worked in a cafe before.*
3 *three months*
4 C *working paid for two hours.*
5 *worried / frightened / scared*
6 A *she has been too busy.*
7 *working at the cash desk / taking money*
8 C *says that he might get a £10 bonus in the future.*

Musterprüfung 2: Reading Comprehension ▶ S. 60 – 66

Young people and holidays
2 D · 4 A · 5 C · 6 E · 7 B

Life in South Africa today
1 C *has changed more than in most countries.*
2 D *couldn't take part in elections and couldn't marry white people.*
3 C *South Africa has eleven official languages.*
4 D *is often spoken as a second language by different ethnic groups.*
5 A *the country celebrates its multicultural society*
6 B *about half of black South Africans are poor.*
7 A *the equipment is not as good as in "white" schools.*
8 A *had more money to spend than it did later.*
9 C *enjoy a better life than they did in 1994.*
10 D *South Africa's government should bring in more changes quickly.*

The D of E expedition
1 *She had to help her friends.*
2 *3 months of volunteering / new sport / special skill*
3 *a longer expedition + you need more food and clothes*
4 *good weather, they didn't get lost*
5 *The ground was hard.*
6 *He lost it in the mud / stepped into mud, only his foot came out.*
7 *Yes, because he had a bad time and didn't complain.*
8 *yes, loyalty to her friends / too proud to drop out*

Musterprüfung 2: Use of language ▶ S. 67 – 70

Mediation
A fun run
a) 1 *öffentliches Rennen über 5 und 10 Kilometer*
  2 A *man darf in Kostüm laufen*
   B *Wagen bringen das Gepäck der Teilnehmer/innen zum Ziel*
   C *es wird empfohlen, keine Musikgeräte mit Kopfhörern beim Laufen zu benutzen*
   D *die Teilnehmer/innen bekommen nach Überqueren der Ziellinie eine Medaille und eine Tüte mit Süßigkeiten*

Sport im Park
b) 1 *It's about free sport in a park in town.*
  2 A *between 8 am and midday on Saturdays*
   B *you can train with a qualified coach*
   C *a range of different sports*
   D *bring your own towel and drinks*
   E *best to book in advance online*

Words and structures

1 C *ever*	8 D *still*
2 D *believe*	9 A *waiting for*
3 C *If*	10 B *just*
4 B *people*	11 D *visiting*
5 D *stopped*	12 C *lots of*
6 B *interested*	13 C *there was*
7 B *about*	14 D *fun*

Musterprüfung 2: Text production ▶ S. 71

Wegen der möglichen Bandbreite an unterschiedlichen Lösungen bei den längeren Schreibaufgaben (150 Wörter) werden für diese Teilaufgaben nur die inhaltlichen Aspekte knapp auf Deutsch skizziert. Siehe ausführlich dazu auch die Hinweise zur Bewertung von Inhalt und Sprache auf S. 36. Generell gilt, dass die folgenden Aspekte in deinem Text berücksichtigt sein sollten, um die volle Punktzahl zu bekommen:

• Du machst wenige Wiederholungen und schweifst nicht vom Thema ab.
• Dein Text lässt sich leicht lesen.
• Dein Text ist klar formuliert und logisch aufgebaut. Du verwendest Bindewörter (Konnektoren) wie *because*, *but*, *so* etc.
• Du verwendest einen vielseitigen Wortschatz und idiomatische Wendungen, z.B. *make a difference*.
• Du bist sicher in der Verwendung verschiedener grammatischer Strukturen.
• Auch wenn bei komplizierten Sätzen vereinzelte Wortschatz- oder Grammatikfehler vorkommen, versteht man, was du sagen willst.

Tipp: Zeig deinen Text doch einem Mitschüler oder einer Mitschülerin und lasse ihn oder sie beurteilen, ob du diese Aspekte berücksichtigt hast. Oder sprich deinen Lehrer oder deine Lehrerin an – sie können es am allerbesten beurteilen.

Notentabelle

Punkte	Note
90 – 100	sehr gut
75 – 89	gut
60 – 74	befriedigend
45 – 59	ausreichend
20 – 44	mangelhaft
0 – 19	ungenügend

2 Answer an email

a) Lies die E-Mail und den Tipp.

> Hi,
> I hope you're OK.
> What did you do at the weekend? Did you do something with your friends?
> And was the weather kind to you?
> And here's an idea: could I come and see you again soon in Germany?
> All the best,
> Josh

> Hi Josh,
> Nice to hear from you.
>
> I had a great weekend, thanks, because I went camping in the mountains with my friend Sam. Dave had wanted to come too, but he didn't have time.
>
> We hiked along muddy valleys, we climbed steep hills and in the evening we cooked on an open fire. Although the weather was awful, it was great fun. The wet nights weren't great, but it was a great feeling when I stood on the the highest mountain that I had ever climbed!
>
> It would be great to see you here again!
> When are your next holidays?
>
> Best wishes, ...

Tipp

> Markiere in der Mail, worüber du schreiben sollst.

b) Lies den Beispieltext.
Er ist zu kurz (nur 104 Wörter). Aber du kannst trotzdem viel daraus lernen.

Inhalt
Sieh dir die Mail von Josh noch einmal an. Markiere die Stellen, die den Inhalt der Aufgabe erfüllen.

Grammatik
Du bekommst Punkte für verschiedene Strukturen und komplexe Satzmuster.
Markiere die Nebensätze bzw. Konjunktionen.
<u>Unterstreiche</u>
– die negative Form von zwei Verben;
– zwei Verben im *past perfect*;
– ein Adjektiv im Superlativ.

Wortschatz
Du bekommst Punkte für abwechslungsreichen Wortschatz.
Notiere hier:
– Verben im *simple past*: _____

– Wie viele verschiedene? _____

– Adjektive _____

– Wie viele verschiedene? _____

– *linking words* (Konnektoren) _____

– Wie viele verschiedene? _____

c) **Jetzt bist du Prüferin oder Prüfer ☺!**
Schau dir noch einmal die Tabelle in **1 e)** an. Dann lies
den Text in **2 b)** noch einmal und entscheide, wie viele
Punkte der Text verdient und warum. (Ignoriere hierbei
dieses Mal die Tatsache, dass der Text zu kurz ist.)

Punkte: _____

Begründung: _____

3 A summary

a) Lies den Text.

My weekend job

Sarah (16) is in trouble with her parents because of her weekend job. She writes about this in her blog.

> **Tipp**
>
> Mache kurze Notizen oder markiere die Stellen im Text, z. B.
> • *what I know about Sarah: at school / needs money: phone, clothes / …*
> • *what I know about the problem: parents against her job: less time for homework / loud music / …*

I hate asking my parents for money. OK, they give me pocket money, but it's never enough for what I need. I pay for my clothes, the contract for my mobile phone, and for a pizza and a drink
5 when I go out with my friends – but that all costs more than what my parents give me every week. That's why I got a job.

It's only a weekend job – and usually I work on Saturday or Sunday, but not both – so I still
10 have time to do homework. I work in a clothes shop in town and I really enjoy it. I have to be there early because I help to clean and organize the shop before the customers arrive. Then I help customers to find what they want and
15 sometimes I even take payment at the till. I'm taking on more responsibility than I have ever had before, and my boss has praised me for being a reliable worker: she knows that I have never arrived late for work.

20 So you would have thought that my parents would be happy. I'm going out into the adult world, I'm showing that I'm responsible and well organized, and of course I don't have to ask them for money so often.

25 I'm really happy about all that. But my parents aren't. They constantly complain about my job.

First they say that I won't do my homework, or that I'll be too tired for school on Monday mornings – even though no teacher has complained about my work. Then they say that the music in the shop is too loud and that working there will destroy my hearing. They have also pointed out that we sell cheap clothes that have been made in Bangladesh, where men, women and children often work in terrible conditions for very little pay. They would prefer it, they say, if I worked in a fair-trade shop that sends more money back to the workers who make the products.

But I have to work where people give me a job, don't I? They forget that I applied for loads of different jobs for about three months without any success. I didn't *choose* to work in this shop – it was the only job offer I got. And anyway, if I worked in a fair-trade shop, I'd be just as tired on a Monday morning, wouldn't I?

I think the real problem is that my parents just can't accept that I'm not a little child any more. They want to control everything I do, and they're afraid that I'll be too independent if I earn my own money. This is the first time we have argued like this – we usually have a good relationship! But I'm determined to keep my job.

b) *Beispiel 1: Wie könnte deine Zusammenfassung aussehen?*
Hier ist ein Beispiel. Lies den Text und die Tipps dazu.
Dann streiche die falschen Alternativen durch.

Wichtige Information – aus dem Text zu schließen.

Bilde komplexe Sätze:
... *because* ...
... *although* ...
... *as* ...
... *but* ...
... *so* ...
... *On the one hand* ...
...

Fasse das Problem in deinen eigenen Worten zusammen.

Sarah has left school / is a student at school and she usually gets on well with / quarrels with her parents. But now she has a weekend job because/so she needs money for her clothes, her phone and for going out with her friends. She works in a clothes shop on a Saturday or Sunday, and she works hard because/ although it means she has to get up early. She arrives on time / is often late, she helps to prepare the shop and she helps the customers. Sometimes she works at the till.

Her boss has said that she is a good worker / is a bit unreliable. But Sarah's parents are unhappy with her job and want her to give it up / don't think that Sarah is a very good worker. They

Diese Information kommt am Ende des Texts vor – ändere die Reihenfolge.

Formuliere eigenständig, z. B. andersherum als im Text: *never late → ?*

c) *Beispiel 2: Wie könnte deine Zusammenfassung aussehen?*
Hier ist ein Beispiel. Lies den Text und die Tipps dazu und bearbeite die Aufgaben in den Kästen.

> Sarah schreibt *enjoy*. Wie kann man das anders ausdrücken?

> In diesem Absatz werden drei Gedanken ausgeführt. Sarahs erster Gedanke ist unterstrichen. Unterstreiche die beiden anderen Gedanken.

> Zu jedem Gedanken wird ein Beispiel genannt, das den Gedanken unterstützt. Unterkringele die Beispiele zu Sarahs ersten beiden Gedanken.
> Kannst du beim dritten Gedanken das Beispiel in deinen eigenen Worten ergänzen?

Sarah really ___ her job. She's grateful for the opportunity to prove that she can work well in the adult world. And of course she's happy to earn some money because she ___ ___ her parents for money.

But Sarah's parents ___ ___ that she has taken a job. They don't like the sort of clothes that she sells and say that she should work in a different kind of shop. And they're worried about her health and fear that she'll get behind with her school work and homework.

Sarah thinks that her parents' reaction is unfair: she didn't choose to work in this shop – it was the only job she could get. She also thinks they're illogical: after all, the effect on her school work would be the same if she worked in a fair-trade shop. And finally, Sarah thinks that her parents' reaction doesn't really have anything to do with her job: they're unhappy, she says, because ___ ___ ___ .

> Wie hat Sarah das ausgedrückt?

> Sarah schreibt *hate asking*. Wie kann man das anders ausdrücken?

> Sarah schreibt *complain about my job*. Wie kann man das anders ausdrücken?

4 Making an argument

a) Lies die Arbeitsanweisungen.

> *You are spending a year at a school in England, where the students are discussing the pros and cons of weekend jobs. You are asked to write an article for the school magazine about this topic and your experience of weekend jobs in Germany.*
> *Include*
> - *some basic information about weekend jobs in Germany*
> - *advantages and disadvantages of weekend jobs*
> - *your opinion (give reasons).*
>
> *Write an article of about 150 words.*

b) Mache dir Notizen zu den drei Punkten in der Aufgabenstellung.
Getting a weekend job is a stupid idea while you are still at school.

– basic information about weekend jobs in Germany: _____

– advantages of weekend jobs: *become independent, ...* _____

– disadvantages of weekend jobs: *less time for homework, ...* _____

– my opinion (with reasons): _____

c) Nun schreibe deinen Text.
  • Beginne mit einer kurzen Einleitung, die klarmacht, worum es hier geht.
  • Führe Argumente für und gegen das Statement auf und belege sie mit Beispielen.
  • Gib deine eigene Meinung.
  • Achte auf deine Sprache.

> **Tipp**
>
> Um die volle Punktzahl zu erhalten, denke daran,
> – zwei bis drei Argumente <u>für und gegen Wochenendjobs</u> anzuführen;
> – dass dein Text logisch aufgebaut, zusammenhängend und klar und verständlich sein muss;
> – einen breiten Wortschatz zu verwenden;
> – auf die gute und sichere Verwendung von Nebensätzen, Konnektoren, Zeiten, modalen Verben, Vergleichen, adverbialen Strukturen und Adverbien zu achten;
> – deinen Text auf Fehler zu überprüfen.

d) Überprüfe deinen Text.
  Hake die aufgelisteten Punkte in der Checkliste ab.

Die Aufgabenstellung ist erfüllt, denn mein Text enthält ...

some basic information about weekend jobs in Germany	☐
advantages and disadvantages of weekend jobs	☐
my opinion (with reasons)	☐

Das Lesen bereitet keine Mühe, denn mein Text zeichnet sich aus durch ...

einen logischen Aufbau	☐
einen breiten Wortschatz	☐
die gute Verwendung von *linking words (and, but, so, because, on the one hand, ...)*	☐
die sichere Verwendung der Grammatik	☐
wenige Fehler	☐

e) Jetzt bist du Prüferin oder Prüfer ☺!
Schau dir noch einmal die Bewertungskriterien in Abschnitt **1 e)** auf Seite 36 an.
Entscheide, wie viele Punkte dein Text verdient und warum.

Punkte: _____

Begründung: _____

Tipps für die Prüfung

Prüfungsvorbereitung

- **Beginne rechtzeitig mit dem Lernen und mache dir einen Lernplan**, bei dem du auch Wiederholungsphasen einplanst. Starte mit Aufgaben, die dir im Unterricht noch schwerfallen. Hake ab, was du bereits erledigt hast.

- **Überlege dir, wo du im Englischen noch grundsätzliche Probleme oder Lücken hast** (z. B. Grammatikprobleme, die immer wieder auftreten). Diese Themen kannst du dann mit den interaktiven Übungen auf www.scook.de gezielt noch einmal wiederholen.

- **Mache dich mit dem Ablauf der Prüfung und mit allen Aufgabenformaten vertraut.** Plane im Vorfeld, wie viel Zeit du für jeden Prüfungsteil und für die Kontrolle zur Verfügung hast.

- **Schreibe dir auf, wann und wo die Prüfung stattfindet**, und plane etwas mehr Zeit für den Weg ein als sonst.

- **Lege alle Materialien am Vorabend der Prüfung bereit** (z. B. funktionstüchtige Stifte, Uhr; Smartphones sind in der Regel nicht erlaubt!).

- **Achte auf ausreichend Schlaf und ein gutes Frühstück.**

Wenn du dich gut vorbereitet hast, kannst du selbstbewusst in die Prüfung gehen!

Während der Prüfung

- **Behalte die Zeit im Blick!** Am besten legst du während der Prüfung eine Uhr auf den Tisch und schaust von Zeit zu Zeit darauf. Wenn du an einer Aufgabe festhängst, gehe lieber erst mal zur nächsten Frage weiter. Nimm dir am Ende einige Minuten Zeit, um deine Antworten noch einmal durchzugehen.

- **Lies die Aufgabenstellung gründlich durch**, bevor du mit der Bearbeitung beginnst. Manchmal enthält eine Aufgabe mehrere Teilaspekte. Markiere sie und übersetze sie dir zur Sicherheit in deine Muttersprache.

- **Nutze deine Chance!** Auch wenn du unsicher bist, ob die Lösung stimmt, so ist es ratsam, die Aufgabe trotzdem zu bearbeiten. So hast du zumindest eine Chance, dass es richtig ist. Kreuzt du keine Lösung an oder lässt die Lücke leer, so bekommst du auf jeden Fall null Punkte.

- **Mache dir bei Schreibaufgaben Notizen, wenn du gut in der Zeit liegst.** Sie können dir helfen, deine Gedanken zu ordnen und deinen Text sinnvoll zu strukturieren. Beachte aber, dass nur dein endgültiger Text in die Bewertung eingeht.

- **Gib deinen Texten eine gute Struktur mit Einleitung, Hauptteil und Schluss.** Beginne jeden neuen Textteil mit einem neuen Absatz.

- **Formuliere klare Sätze.** Vermeide es, komplizierte deutsche Sätze wortwörtlich ins Englische zu übersetzen. Formuliere möglichst mit deinen eigenen Worten, es sei denn, die Aufgabenstellung verlangt ein Zitat aus dem Text (z. B. „Quote from the text.", „Give examples from the text.").

- **Kontrolliere am Ende**, was du geschrieben hast. Achte besonders auf Vollständigkeit, die Rechtschreibung, die Zeitformen deiner Verben und den Satzbau.

Wir wünschen dir viel Erfolg für deine Prüfung!

ABSCHLUSS-
PRÜFUNGS-
TRAINER

Hessen

Musterprüfungen

A Listening comprehension

Part 1

A tour guide: Bo-Kaap – a special district in Cape Town, South Africa

11

> • *Listen to the guide and tick (✓) the right statements.*
> • *There is only one possible answer per statement*

(4 points)

1 The Bo-Kaap mosque was built ...

   A ☐ at the end of the 18th century.

   B ☐ a hundred years ago.

   C ☐ in 1974.

2 The people who ruled Cape Town back then ...

   A ☐ were Asian.

   B ☐ built the Bo-Kaap mosque.

   C ☐ were Europeans.

A street in Bo-Kaap

3 People from India and South-East Asia came ...

   A ☐ to work in South Africa.

   B ☐ to visit South Africa.

   C ☐ to sell things to South Africans.

4 Over one million people in South Africa ...

   A ☐ are Muslim.

   B ☐ are Asian.

   C ☐ are from Bo-Kaap.

A special plane

12

> • *Listen to the report and tick (✓) the right statements.*
> • *There is only one possible answer per statement.*

(4 points)

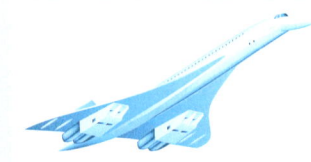

1 The report is about a plane that was made in ...

   A ☐ two European countries.

   B ☐ Britain and the USA.

   C ☐ the USA.

2 The plane could fly ...

   A ☐ almost as fast as the speed of sound.

   B ☐ at the speed of sound.

   C ☐ twice as fast as the speed of sound.

3 Its fastest flight from London to New York was ...

   A ☐ one hour and fifty-three minutes.

   B ☐ two hours and twenty-three minutes.

   C ☐ two hours and fifty-three minutes.

4 The big problem with the plane was ...

   A ☐ it was too fast.

   B ☐ it did not sell well.

   C ☐ it was not safe.

Part 2: Adverts

13

- Listen to the adverts. Match each advert with one person.
- Write the correct names in the chart.
- Be careful – there is one more person than you need.

(7 points)

> I try to keep healthy. That's a big factor in my food and activities.
> **Sam**

> Typical! Some people don't take recycling seriously enough!
> **Anna**

> I want to work in an old people's home.
> **Rashid**

> I strongly believe that all cosmetics should be ethically sourced.
> **Grace**

> I work till 6 pm, but I'd like to do something after that where I can meet people.
> **Livvy**

> I don't understand it! How can people be so stupid? Why be lazy and risk your life?
> **Wayne**

> I'm looking for a job that is a bit different, maybe at sea.
> **Katy**

> I don't really enjoy my work. Time for a change, I think.
> **LIZ**

Advert 1:	Advert 2:	Advert 3:	Advert 4:
Advert 5:	Advert 6:	Advert 7:	

Part 3: A presentation about William Shakespeare

> • *Listen to the presentation and note down the information about William Shakespeare.*
> • *Fill in only one detail per box.*

(10 points)

William Shakespeare
(1564–1616)

1 Why William Shakespeare is famous	
2 The year he was born	
3 Names of his parents	
4 How old William was when he married	
5 What happened to William's son	
6 Where he lived most of his life	
7 What you can see in Henley Street in Stratford on Avon	
8 What you can see in Stratford on Avon's town hall	
9 What the Globe Theatre looks like	
10 What is special about watching a play here	

B Reading comprehension

Good health in Australia?

This article is from a British fitness and health magazine.

1

Open any travel brochure with flights to Australia and happy groups of athletic-looking young people smile at you from its pages. Search Australia's TV channels and slim, healthy individuals beam at you from the screen, and not only in the adverts. The lifesavers featured in Reality TV shows like Bondi Beach and Surf Patrol have one thing in common: they are slim, healthy and agile.

2

No wonder Australia is so popular with emigrants from Europe. More Brits begin a new life abroad in Australia than in any other country – over 200,000 between 2010 and 2015. During this period Australia was three times more popular than the USA, for example. And the emigrants' happy stories of sunshine, barbecues, surfing, snorkelling and beach volleyball contrast with our indoor existence back home. The Australian sun, we think, encourages Australians to keep fit; our dismal weather gives us a good excuse for sit at home, eat and put on weight.

3

And yet the reality is different. Australia is in fact experiencing an explosion in obesity rates. Between 2014 and 2015, two in every three Australians were considered medically overweight or obese (overweight is defined as having some excess body fat, while obese is defined as having so much excess body fat that it has a negative effect on health). In today's obesity rankings, Australia is ahead of France and Germany. And as excess weight is a risk factor for heart disease, type 2 diabetes and some cancers, the worry is that the country will see a dramatic increase in these diseases.

4

The reasons for the problem are basically a bad diet and a lack of exercise. Only half of all Australians consume the amount of fruit recommended in the national guidelines, only seven percent meet the target for vegetables. And while just over half of all Australians take part in 150 minutes of moderate physical activity per week, as recommended (or 75 minutes of vigorous activity), just under half do not. This includes almost 15 percent who do no physical activity at all – and these figures exclude those over 64 years old.

5

Australia is of course by no means alone with this problem. It is a feature of modern life in many countries, and no country anywhere in the world has yet found a way of reducing its obesity rates. However, the huge rise comes as a particularly nasty surprise in Australia because it contrasts so starkly with the self-image of fitness and health. In future, it will be more and more difficult for the makers of the holiday brochures and TV series to find the slim and healthy Australians for their holiday photos and TV series.

> • *Match the five correct headings to the parts of the text (1–5).*
> • *Be careful – there are two headings more than you need.*

(5 points)

A The opposite of slim

B It's what you (don't) eat and do

C Too long in hospital

D Attractive for emigrants

E Australia in the media

F Less easy to find people without a weight problem

G A problem caused by sunshine

part of the text	1	2	3	4	5
heading					

High-rise living in Britain

The following text is from the lifestyle section of a British newspaper.

Tower block in London

Apartment blocks have long had a bad press in Britain. People think of the 1960s tower blocks that were usually built for people in lower-paid jobs. The flats were small and the entrances
5   were dark and dirty, full of litter and graffiti. The lifts didn't work. People only lived in these high-rise apartment blocks if they had no alternative, and in the last few decades, councils in several cities have destroyed as many of them as they
10 could.

Of course, the tower blocks have always had their fans. Residents often feel safer than in a house because nobody can climb through the window of a flat on the 16th floor: in fact, no-
15 body can even look in, so you don't have to draw your curtains at night. And the flats are largely free from mice. These voices were long in the minority, but not any more. Flats are popular once more. Why is this?

20 One reason is that houses are simply costing too much for many people, and building taller makes for cheaper homes. Another is that while people used to dream of having a house and garden, new trends in working hours mean
25 that people no longer have time for garden work. Instead, they prefer to have a few plants on a balcony.

What's more, the apartments going up today are large and airy, and attract people on good incomes. CCTV cameras keep the entrances safe, and companies are employed to clean the corridors and maintain the lifts. Some of these modern flats are built as 'pods' – that is to say, each flat is built as a self-contained unit, with bathrooms and kitchen equipped to a high standard, and the pods are then placed one on top of the other. This is often less costly than traditional building techniques, and customers can make their choice of equipment as they would do if they were buying a car.

Families with children still usually prefer to live in a house with a front door, a back door and a garden. Parents can keep an eye on their children in the garden, and it's often easier to get to know your neighbours by chatting over the garden fence than by sharing the lift up the 8th floor. But a recent report has challenged the widely-held view that high-rise blocks offer a less healthy environment. Experts from the University of Bern in Switzerland found that people who live on the 8th floor or above are likely to live longer than those who live on the lower floors. Those living higher up, they claim, are 35% less likely to die from heart disease – partly because walking up more stairs keeps people fitter. There is also less air pollution on the higher floors and people are also less affected by traffic noise.

The apartment blocks being built today are here to stay.

1 The flats in the 1960s tower blocks …

- **A** ☐ were often very attractive.
- **B** ☐ were not always clean, but at least had good lifts.
- **C** ☐ were for poor families.
- **D** ☐ were for richer families.

2 In the last few years councils in a number of cities have …

- **A** ☐ taken down their 1960s tower blocks.
- **B** ☐ modernised their 1960s tower blocks.
- **C** ☐ built more tower blocks like those from the 1960s.
- **D** ☐ sold their 1960s tower blocks.

3 Some people today feel that tower block flats are …

- **A** ☐ full of insects.
- **B** ☐ safe because burglars cannot break in so easily.
- **C** ☐ dangerous because you could fall out of the windows.
- **D** ☐ too dark when the curtains are closed at night.

4 Flats are becoming more popular again because …

- **A** ☐ people have more money, so they can pay the higher rents.
- **B** ☐ people want to live higher off the ground floor.
- **C** ☐ they are easier to take care of.
- **D** ☐ they sometimes have a nice garden.

5 More and more of the flats are now …

A ☐ smaller than before.

B ☐ better quality than those built in the 1960s.

C ☐ built for older people.

D ☐ built exclusively for young people.

6 People in these modern high-rise flats …

A ☐ can only meet other residents in the lift.

B ☐ can't see who comes in and goes out of their building.

C ☐ don't have to pay anything for the extra facilities.

D ☐ don't need to worry about cleaning the communal areas.

7 The flats that are built as pods …

A ☐ are often cheaper than other flats.

B ☐ have poor quality kitchens and bathrooms.

C ☐ can only be used at ground floor level.

D ☐ all look exactly the same on the inside.

8 The text argues that most British families …

A ☐ now want to live in a nice modern flat.

B ☐ never invite their neighbours in their garden.

C ☐ like to see their children when they are playing.

D ☐ get to know their neighbours in the lift.

9 What most people believe is that …

A ☐ houses aren't good for the environment.

B ☐ flats aren't good for the environment.

C ☐ living in a flat is better for you.

D ☐ living in a house is better for you.

10 According to a recent report, living on higher floors in apartment blocks …

A ☐ helps against heart disease.

B ☐ is dangerous because the air is very dirty.

C ☐ is louder than living on the lower floors.

D ☐ is bad for your knees because of the stairs.

My first journey abroad

Paul, an English teenager, writes about a fantastic experience on his first evening in a different country.

I was never good at foreign languages at school. My marks in German and French were awful, and as a result of this terrible experience of learning languages I was afraid of travelling abroad. How, I thought, could I find the way if all the signs were in a language that I couldn't understand?

So when Phil, my best friend at school, suggested a cycling holiday in France, I first said "No." But he kept trying to persuade me and I knew I would feel guilty if he went alone. So in the end I said "OK, I'll go!" So in mid-August, after we had both worked in a fast-food cafe for a month to earn some money, we travelled down to Dover and put our bikes on the ferry to France.

When we arrived in Calais, in France, we had to drive on the right. That was scary, and we soon got lost. I didn't dare ask the way because I knew that I wouldn't understand the answer. But then Phil asked a woman – and she answered in English! I began to feel better. If people in France could speak English, I had nothing to be afraid of ...

Imagine my disappointment, then, when we arrived at our hostel in Calais and found that we were sharing a four-bed dormitory with two guys from Serbia who spoke no English at all. "This will be a very quiet evening," I thought.

But then one of the guys came over and said something, pointed at Phil and smiled. Then he said it again. I tried to explain that I couldn't understand Serbian, but he just smiled. He pointed at himself and said "Filip." And then he pointed at Phil and said the same word again – and I suddenly realized what he meant. "Ah, you're both called Philip," I said. "He Philip," I added, pointing at Phil, "and you Filip," pointing

Philip & Filip

at him. And he cheered. I felt better. Filip pointed at his friend and said "Dragan," and Dragan took out a bar of chocolate and shared it with us.

Then Filip said something much longer. I tried to recognize some words, but I couldn't. Filip took out a pen and drew on a piece of paper. Was it a cushion? Was it a hat? If so, it was a strange hat. Then he drew the Union Jack. And a woman. And a big building – it looked like a palace. And suddenly I shouted "The Queen! Elizabeth!" Filip nodded and laughed and we gave each other five.

And so it went on with words, and drawings, and acting things out. And finally we understood what he wanted to say: Filip and Dragan had been to London and they had seen the Queen. When we got the whole sentence, we all cheered. Then Dragan took out some food from his bag and we all ate together. We felt great.

It had taken us half an hour to understand Filip's sentence – and it wasn't a very important sentence. But that didn't matter. He had communicated, we had understood. Language had brought us closer together.

> • *Answer the questions.*

1 Why did Paul not want to leave England? (1 point)

_____

2 Why did Paul agree to go to France? (1 point)

_____

3 How did Phil and Paul pay for the holiday? (1 point)

_____

4 What was Phil and Paul's accommodation in Calais? (1 point)

_____

5 What did the Serbian boy first communicate to Paul? (1 point)

_____

6 How did Filip communicate? (two details / 2 points)

_____

7 How did the boys celebrate when Phil and Paul understood Filip's second communication? (1 point)

_____

> • *You cannot find the answers to the following questions directly in the text:*

8 How do you think Paul felt when he and Phil got off the ferry in Calais? (1 point)

_____

9 What sort of hat do you think Filip drew? (1 point)

_____

C Use of language

1 Mediation

An email from a cousin

Deine deutsche Freundin Carola bekommt eine Mail von ihrer Cousine Lucy in England.

Subject: Job in Germany?

Hi Carola,

I hope you remember me: I'm your cousin Lucy, in Bedford, in England. We last met at a family reunion almost five years ago – remember?

I'm writing to you because I'll be leaving school this summer. I'm working here in Bedford in July and August, but instead of going to college in September, I want to get more experience in a job. And I wondered if I could work in Germany for a few weeks between September and Christmas?

What I'm really interested in is the theatre – not only acting, but sound and lighting, or helping with the costumes, as I'm quite good at sewing. Basically, I wonder whether you could help me to find any job in a theatre? I don't expect to be paid – I've saved up some money, so I could pay for my flight and for a room somewhere (but of course if job was in Limburg I might be able to stay with you?).

Don't worry if you can't help – but if you can, I'd be really grateful!

Love to you and your family,
Lucy

---

a) Carola, die Schwierigkeiten mit dem Fach Englisch hat, bittet dich, ihr zu erklären, um was es in Lucys E-Mail geht.

1 Nenne auf Deutsch das Hauptanliegen, warum Lucy die E-Mail geschrieben hat (vollständige Sätze sind nicht notwendig):

_____

_____

2 Nenne ihr vier weitere wichtige Informationen auf Deutsch (vollständige Sätze sind nicht notwendig):

A _____

B _____

C _____

D _____

b) Carola hat nun diese Auskunft für Lucy gefunden. Sie bittet dich, ihr zu helfen, die Hauptinformationen auf Englisch zusammenzufassen.

---

www.geraldtheater.de/praktikum

Praktikum am Gerald Theater

Das Angebot an Praktika im Gerald Theater ist wunderbar vielfältig. Die Aufgabenbereiche umfassen neben Schauspiel und Dramaturgie auch Ton- und Beleuchtungstechnik, Tischlerei, Schneiderei, Bühnenbild, Marketing und Kartenvertrieb sowie „Front-of-House"-Aufgaben wie Arbeit im Café, Garderobe usw.

Du erhältst auf jeden Fall Einblicke in den künstlerischen Entstehungsprozess einer Inszenierung. Theatererfahrung ist kein Muss, vielmehr interessiert uns dein volles Engagement.

Grundsätzlich müssen Praktikanten im Gerald Theater mindestens 15 Jahre alt sein.

Praktika sind normalerweise zwei Wochen lang. In Ausnahmefällen können Praktika von maximal drei Monaten angeboten werden. Die Aufgaben, Tagesabläufe und Arbeitszeiten können je nach Abteilung sehr unterschiedlich sein. Arbeit am Abend und am Wochenende kann verlangt werden, aber ein Maximum von 35 Stunden in der Woche wird nicht überschnitten.

Das Praktikum ist unvergütet, Praktikanten bekommen aber Freikarten für alle Produktionen im Gerald Theater in einem Zeitraum von einem Monat, unabhängig von der Dauer des Praktikums.

---

1 Notiere dir zunächst auf Englisch die Hauptinformation in diesem Text, die Lucy interessieren könnte:

_____

_____

2 Notiere auf Englisch fünf weitere wichtige Informationen, die Lucy interessieren könnten (vollständige Sätze sind nicht notwendig):

A _____

B _____

C _____

D _____

E _____

2 Words and structures

The Everglades

> • *Read the text, then choose the correct words from the box to fill in the gaps.*
> • *Use each word once only. There are more words than you need.*

(14 points)

completed • drying • from • how • huge • inhabitants • pass • polluted • quickly • replaced • south • their • there • what • which • who • worse

The wetlands of the Everglades in the **1**_____ of the state of Florida are famous for **2**_____ alligators, snakes, turtles and other wildlife, **3**_____ tourists can sometimes catch sight of from airboats or from specially-provided hiking trails. Visitor centres show alligators feeding and inform tourists about **4**_____ the alligators' environment is endangered. In fact, the Everglades are facing **5**_____ environmental issues. Its lakes and rivers are **6**_____ by dirty waste water from the city of Miami. And pets released into the Everglades by **7**_____ of the city have become a danger to the original wildlife. But the biggest headache of all is that the wetlands are **8**_____ out. This is partly because, in the 1960ies, the slow-flowing Kissimmee River was **9**_____ by a dead straight canal that takes the water away too **10**_____. And what makes it **11**_____ is that the U.S. Highway 41, which was **12**_____ in 1928, cuts through 275 miles of the Everglades from east to west on a wall of earth. This prevents water **13**_____ flowing into the southern part of the Everglades. It has now been decided that parts of the canal will be filled in to allow the water to flow in the slower river. And a mile-long stretch of Highway 41 will be made into a bridge to allow water to **14**_____ under it.

5

10

15

20

25

30

55

D Text production

> • *Choose one of the following tasks and write about 150 words.*
> • *Count your words and write the number at the end of the text.*

(25 points)

What is the story behind the picture?

> *Write a text and include at least four of the following aspects:*
> • *Who is it?*
> • *When and where is it?*
> • *How did the person get here?*
> • *What will happen next?*
> • *What are your/their thoughts?*

The best day in my life

> *Write a text and include at least four of the following aspects:*
> • *When and where was it?*
> • *Who was important on the day, and why?*
> • *What happened?*
> • *How did you feel during the day and afterwards?*
> • *Why was the day so special?*

A Listening comprehension

Part 1

A report about St Kilda

> • *Listen to the report.*
> • *Answer the questions.*

(4 points)

1 How far away from Scotland is St Kilda?

_____

2 The inhabitants of St Kilda grew some food.
What else did they eat?

_____

3 What happened to the last inhabitants of St Kilda?

_____

4 Where do you sleep if you stay on the island of Hirta?

_____

A report about Wales

> • *Listen to the report and tick (✓) the right statements.*
> • *There is only one possible answer per statement.*

(4 points)

1 The Welsh language is ...

   A ☐ a dialect of English.

   B ☐ different from English, but with
many similarities.

   C ☐ not like English at all.

2 People who live in Brittany in north-west France ...

   A ☐ speak a language like the Welsh language.

   B ☐ use the Welsh word for Britain.

   C ☐ use a few Welsh words in their own language.

3 The Welsh language is …

A ☐ a majority language in Wales.

B ☐ a minority language in Wales.

C ☐ spoken by less than 5% of the total Welsh population.

4 The Welsh language is most widely spoken …

A ☐ the south and west of Wales.

B ☐ the mountains in the centre of Wales.

C ☐ the north and west of Wales.

Part 2

Radio notices

You will hear five notices given on the radio.

🎧 **17**

- *Look at the different boxes below.*
- *Choose the right topic for each notice.*
- *There is one more topic than you need.*
- *Listen to the notices twice.*

(5 points)

A new system	**Don't spread disease**	**Healthy hot drinks**
Think of your weight	**Safe toys?**	**Dispose of your rubbish responsibly**

Notice 1 _____

Notice 2 _____

Notice 3 _____

Notice 4 _____

Notice 5 _____

Part 3

First job

Tom is looking for work.
You will hear Tom talking at a job fair and then with his employer, Linda, at his place of work.
You will hear the conversations twice.

🎧 **18**

- *Tick (✓) the right statements and fill the gaps.*

1 The sort of work that Tom wants is

_____ . (2 points)

2 The first employer doesn't offer Tom a job because …

  A ☐ Tom has never worked in a cafe before.

  B ☐ Tom is too young.

  C ☐ Tom is still a student at school. (1 point)

3 The length of time that Tom has been looking for work is

_____ . (2 points)

4 Linda offers Tom the opportunity to see if he will like the work by …

  A ☐ working unpaid for a day.

  B ☐ working paid for a day.

  C ☐ working paid for two hours. (1 point)

5 When Linda tells Tom that she wants to talk with him, he feels

_____ . (2 points)

6 Linda tells Tom that she hadn't talked with him much because …

  A ☐ she has been too busy.

  B ☐ managers should not talk too much with their workers.

  C ☐ she has been away. (1 point)

7 Tom's work in the Happy Diner restaurant has included preparing food and

_____ . (2 points)

8 Linda is happy with Tom's work, so she …

  A ☐ offers him a bonus of £10 a week.

  B ☐ pays him a single payment of £10.

  C ☐ says that he might get a £10 bonus in the future. (1 point)

B Reading comprehension

Young people and holidays

> • Decide which of the different kinds of holidays described in the texts (1–7) is the most suitable for the young people below (A–E).

(5 points)

A		For me, holidays are about discovering new places. I love city centres packed with ancient buildings, monuments and churches, and I love museums and exhibitions. It's not always easy to find people with the same interests, but when I do meet people with similar interests, we have a great time. **Robyn**
B		In my holidays I want to do something active. I like cycling and badminton, but I'm open to trying out new sports and activities. I don't mind shared accommodation (though I'm not so keen on camping) and I like places with staff with the expertise and equipment to show you how to tackle new activities. **Paddy**
C		I want to relax in my holidays, with time for myself, time to remember who I really am. For this I need to be in the country, in touch with nature. However, I really don't like long walks. I need time for thinking, for reading, and sometimes just to curl up near a warm fire and not have to think of anything. **Robert**
D		When I go on holiday I want everything to be easy. I want to be lazy, to relax in the sun, with meals and drinks when I want them. I'm not a great swimmer, but sea bathing is a must. I like lively places where there's something going on, and I don't mind the noise. **Becky**
E		I broke up with my boyfriend a few months ago, so I'm going on my own and I want to meet lots of people. I want to go abroad, but I don't really like organizing things, so I like packages in which the travel, accommodation and visits are all included. But I can't stand loud hotels! I like walking around towns on my own, and watching people, rather than having guided tours. **Hannah**

1   Jump on a train and explore Europe with Interrail. With your Interrail Pass, all train travel is free. Choose 5 days of travel within a period of 15 days for 206 euros*, or 7 days of travel within a month for 253 euros*. Or travel every day within a month for 493 euros*. It's up to you.

*Prices quoted are for travellers aged up to 27.

2   Marbella Bella Hotel Review
Large modern hotel located in Marbella, on the sun-drenched Costa del Sol in the south of Spain. 10 minutes from the beach and 5 minutes from the main street with shops, cafes, restaurants, etc. This hotel is for party people, a place to make friends. The rooms are OK: clean and quite big. The pool is nice and big and has plenty of loungers. But be aware that it is often quite noisy as people are coming back from parties all night.

3   Take a holiday in Adventure Land! Based in Robin Hood country, we offer activities, from rowing to table tennis, from archery to quad driving. And the price of your holiday includes your accommodation, full use of the surrounding forest area and unlimited access to our Exotic Swimming Paradise – where it never rains, because it is under an enormous glass roof!

4   Join us on a weekend of Prague for culture vultures. The package includes your flights and accommodation, all entrance fees and the services of an expert guide. On Saturday we have a coach tour of the city, we visit the Castle and the Archbishop's Palace, and attend a concert, ballet or opera. And on Sunday we have a guided tours of the Tyn Church and more famous sights. A great opportunity to discover Prague in the company of like-minded people.

5   Visitors come to our monastery in a beautiful quiet valley just for a night, or for a week or more. Some just Bed and Breakfast, others take part in a 'retreat': a time to be alone or in a group, in silence or taking part in our daily prayer in our peaceful gardens. You can also speak in confidence to our Retreat Director. All our visitors leave feeling rested, renewed and fitter for the lives they go back to.

6   Coach trip to the Low Countries. Join us on an 8-day tour of Belgium and the Netherlands, where you will be free to explore towns like Bruges, Brussels, Amsterdam and Delft in any way you wish. The package includes the ferry, luxury coach travel, and half-board accommodation in 4 or 5 stars hotels (drinks not included). The price does not include your travel to Hull or entrance fees to museums, etc.

7   Come to Levisham Park Centre in the Yorkshire Moors National Park for great outdoor activities in the natural environment: rock climbing, hill walking, camping, sailing, orienteering, canoeing and kayaking, caving, and many more. Accommodation is in 8-bed dormitories. Our trainers are fully qualified and have many years of experience with working with young people.

Life in South Africa today

> • *Read the text and tick (✓) the right statements.*

(10 points)

Few countries have changed as radically in the last twenty-five years as South Africa. Before the country's first free election in 1994, everything depended on the colour of your skin.
5 Under a system called apartheid, black and white people lived in different zones, went to different schools, relaxed on different beaches and used different public toilets. Black people could not vote, and marriages between black
10 and white people were forbidden.

The election of Nelson Mandela, South Africa's first black president, in 1994 put an end to all that. South Africans – black, white and Asian – now enjoy equal rights. Nine African
15 languages, including Zulu (the first language of over 20% of South Africans!), have joined English and Afrikaans (a language brought to South Africa by Dutch settlers) as official languages. So most parents can send their children to
20 schools which teach in their own language. English is a minority language in terms of first language, but it's the language of trade and the media, and the language that allows people of different ethnic groups to communicate. It is
25 this wide range of cultures, languages and ethnic backgrounds, rather than the climate or the sometimes colourful way of dressing, that has earned South Africa the nickname of the Rainbow Nation.

30 But changes for the better are coming too slowly for many black South Africans. The white population (nine percent of the total population) still owns a larger proportion of the country's wealth than black South Africans (80 percent
35 of the population). True, a few black people have become rich, but 54 percent of the black population live in poverty, compared to 0.8 percent of the white population.

This inequality is evident in education.
40 Schools in mostly white areas of the country are better equipped with computers and toilets than schools in mostly black areas. Schools teaching in one of the official African languages often find it difficult to employ teachers who
45 can speak their language. And as many parents die young, students often have to leave school to look after younger brothers and sisters.

South Africa's economy is now growing by less than two percent a year, which is a lower increase than in the first years of the 21st centu- 50 ry. This means that the government now has less money for improving schools and social conditions.

But South Africa's problems should not be exaggerated. The economy is the biggest in 55 Africa after Nigeria, and incomes per person are among the highest in Africa. South Africa's middle class grew by an extraordinary 250% between 2004 and 2012. However, while conditions have generally improved for most 60 people, and blacks can now go onto beaches and into bars that were once reserved for whites, life is still hard for many black South Africans. The gap between the standard of living of black and white South Africans is as large as ever, so it's 65 not surprising that more and more blacks are becoming impatient for more change.

1 The writer's opinion is that life in South Africa ...

    A ☐ has changed less than in most countries.

    B ☐ has changed about the same as in most countries.

    C ☐ has changed more than in most countries.

    D ☐ has not changed much in the last few years.

2 Under apartheid black people ...

    A ☐ could take part in elections, but couldn't marry white people.

    B ☐ could take part in elections, but couldn't go to the same beaches as white people.

    C ☐ couldn't take part in elections, but could marry white people.

    D ☐ couldn't take part in elections and couldn't marry white people.

3 As far as languages are concerned, it is true that ...

    A ☐ schools teach in English or Afrikaans.

    B ☐ a majority of South Africans speak Zulu.

    C ☐ South Africa has eleven official languages.

    D ☐ Afrikaans is a language that was first spoken by black South Africans.

4 The text says that English ...

    A ☐ is spoken by a small majority of South Africans as a first language.

    B ☐ is a dying language in South Africa.

    C ☐ is now less important than Zulu online, on radio and on TV.

    D ☐ is often spoken as a second language by different ethnic groups.

5 South Africa is sometimes called the Rainbow Nation because ...

    A ☐ the country celebrates its multicultural society.

    B ☐ people wear very colourful clothes.

    C ☐ it has a climate with a high number of rainbows.

    D ☐ rainbows are important in traditional stories.

6 The situation today, according to the text, is that ...

    A ☐ black South Africans now have more money than white South Africans.

    B ☐ about half of black South Africans are poor.

    C ☐ only 0.8 percent of the white population are still rich.

    D ☐ most South Africans feel that conditions are changing fast enough.

7 Schools in mostly black areas are at a disadvantage because ...

    A ☐ the equipment is not as good as in "white" schools.

    B ☐ it's hard to find English-speaking staff.

    C ☐ the students protest against inequality.

    D ☐ they are in the city centres.

8 In the first years of the 21st century, the South African government ...

    A ☐ had more money to spend than it did later.

    B ☐ could not spend as much money as it did later.

    C ☐ could spend less on schools than today.

    D ☐ was still trying to enforce apartheid.

9 Today, South Africans ...

    A ☐ have the biggest economy in Africa.

    B ☐ earn less than in most African countries.

    C ☐ enjoy a better life than they did in 1994.

    D ☐ all have more or less the same standard of living.

10 The author of this text thinks that ...

    A ☐ South Africa's government should not bring in any more changes.

    B ☐ South Africans had a better life under apartheid.

    C ☐ black South Africans have an easy life today.

    D ☐ South Africa's government should bring in more changes quickly.

The D of E expedition

Dreamings is a book about a girl's adventurous summer in Britain.
In this excerpt, Keira is on an expedition with her friends.

- *Read the text and answer the questions.*

I put down my rucksack and almost fell to the ground. I was so tired that I just closed my eyes and wanted to forget everything. But then I heard my friend Katherine's voice. "Hey, lazybones!" she said. "Get up and come and help us put up this tent." And somehow I found the strength to get up and help my friends. I couldn't let them down.

It was the second night of our D-of-E expedition. D-of-E stands for Duke of Edinburgh – he's the Queen's husband. Back in 1956, he started a challenge to give young people a taste of adventure out in the country. You take part at one of three levels: bronze, silver and gold – like the medals in the Olympics.

For the lowest level, bronze, you have to do four different things. For example, you have to volunteer, which means spending three months helping in your village library, maybe, or visiting and chatting with people in an old people's home. You also have to spend three months doing a new sport or physical activity (your normal sports lessons at school don't count!), and practise a special skill for three months – like playing a musical instrument, or learning more about birds or trees. And then there's the expedition: a 25 to 30 kilometre hike, spread over two days, which you do in a team with friends. You have to carry your own camping equipment and food and clothes, and cook for yourselves. And you have to read a map.

But Katherine, Joss, Ibrahim and I had already done the bronze the year before, so we were doing the Silver Award. That's like the bronze, but with longer periods of volunteering, sport and skill work, and in particular a longer expedition. For silver, you walk for three days, and camp for two nights. You carry your tent and equipment as for bronze, but more things to eat and to wear. That makes your rucksack heavier.

Katherine was our map reader, and on our first day she guided us along paths through woods and across fields without getting us lost.

The sun was shining, and we kept up a good speed. In the evening we put up the tents, and cooked a simple pasta meal. We felt proud of being a good team!

I didn't sleep too well because the ground wasn't exactly soft – but at least the tent didn't fall down. But in the morning we woke up to rain, and it rained while we took our tents down, so they made our rucksacks heavier. Then the map got wet, Katherine found it hard to read it, and we got lost in a very muddy valley.

We weren't feeling too happy, and then the calamity happened. Ibrahim stepped into really deep mud, and when he pulled his foot out his shoe stayed in the mud and he lost it. We all tried to help find the shoe, and all got really dirty, but it was no good. All we could do was tie a plastic bag around Ibrahim's foot to try to keep it dry. Poor Ibrahim! He had to walk another three miles like this, and he never complained.

Because we lost our way so often, we ended up walking further than we thought – we walked for over six hours. That's why I was so exhausted. I had never walked as far in my whole life.

And when I woke up the next morning, I lay in my tent and wondered if I would be strong enough for the challenges of the day ahead. Would I have to drop out?

1   Why didn't Keira just fall asleep at the end of the second days' hike?   (1 point)

_____

2   Name one thing apart from the expedition that you have to do for the bronze D of E award.   (1 point)

_____

3   Why is your rucksack heavier for silver level than for bronze level?   (2 points)

_____

4   What went well on the first day of Keira's expedition?   (2 points)

_____

5   Why didn't Keira get a good night's sleep?   (1 point)

_____

6   How did Ibrahim lose his shoe?   (1 point)

_____

> • *You cannot find the answers to the following questions directly in the text:*

7   Do you think that Keira admired Ibrahim? Why (not?)   (1 point)

_____

8   Do you think Keira will continue with her hike? Why (not?)   (1 point)

_____

C Use of language

1 Mediation

A fun run

Du bist Mitglied eines Sportvereins. Aus Neugier habt ihr einen Sportverein in eurer Partnerstadt in England gefragt, was für Sportereignisse für die Öffentlichkeit dort veranstaltet werden. Als Teil der Antwort kommt diese Broschüre.

The Great Fun Run

Our annual Great Fun Run will again take place over a 5 km or a 10 km course and is open to people of all ages (parents are responsible for their children).

This is a Fun Run, so you are welcome to run in fancy dress. However, please bear in mind the weather conditions and remember you may need to drink more if wearing fancy dress.

The run starts at 9.15 am in Kings Park, but please arrive at least an hour early to allow yourself time to warm up and use the toilet facilities before the race begins. You can also put your belongings on baggage trucks at Kings Park: they will be taken to the finish line where you can collect them.

Free water will be available along the course of the run.

Personal music-playing devices are not banned, but we recommend that you do not use them while you run. You should be able to hear what is happening around you, including any emergency services that may be operating.

10 km and 5 km participants will receive a finisher T-shirt, a medal and a small bag of goodies when they cross the finish line.

Good luck and have fun!

a)   Die Mitglieder deines Sportvereins bitten dich, ihnen zu erklären, um was es in der Broschüre geht.

1   Nenne zuerst auf Deutsch die Hauptinformation der Broschüre.

_____

_____

2   Nenne ihnen vier weitere wichtige Informationen auf Deutsch
(vollständige Sätze sind nicht notwendig):

A _____

B _____

C _____

D _____

Im Gegenzug findet ihr im Sportverein diese Infos über öffentlichen Sport in eurer Stadt.

Sport im Park

Du brauchst kein Fitnessstudio, um dich in der Stadt fit zu halten! Komm einfach jeden Samstagvormittag in den Konrad-Adenauer-Park und trainiere kostenlos mit einem unserer ausgebildeten Trainer.

Der Kreisjugendring organisiert dort zwischen 8 Uhr und 12 Uhr ein umfassendes Programm für interessierte Menschen jeden Alters. Von Zirkeltraining über Tai-Chi und Zumba bis hin zu Pilates und Yoga ist alles im Angebot. Bring einfach bequeme Kleidung, ein Handtuch oder eine Matte und etwas zu trinken mit. Wir sorgen dann für Bälle, Netze usw., für motivierende Musik und die richtigen Bewegungsabläufe.

Sport im Park ist gratis, aber es ist ratsam, sich online zu registrieren und einen festen Platz zu buchen (pro Gruppe nicht mehr als 20 Teilnehmer). Mit etwas Glück kann man aber auch spontan einen Platz finden, falls ein Angemeldeter nicht erschienen ist. Es lohnt sich also, einfach vorbeizuschauen!

Sport im Park wird auch in den Ferien angeboten, nicht jedoch bei Regen.

www.sport-im-park.de

b) Du möchtest diese Infos dem englischen Sportverein weitergeben.

1 Notiere dir zunächst auf Englisch die Hauptinformation, die die Leser/innen interessieren könnte.

_____

_____

2 Notiere auf Englisch fünf weitere wichtige Informationen, die die Sportler/innen in eurer Partnerstadt interessieren könnten (vollständige Sätze sind nicht notwendig):

A _____

B _____

C _____

D _____

E _____

2 Words and structures

> • *Read the text and tick (✓) the correct answer.*

(14 points)

I've just come back from the coolest, the most brilliant, the most totally AMAZING holiday I've **1**_____ had! Ten days in Canada and the USA with Mum, Dad and my sister Louise. This was my first trip to North America – and I must go back! The thing you read all the time, but never actually **2**_____ until you're there, is that these countries are just SO BIG! You can't "see" them in a few days. Here are a few notes about the holiday.

3_____ you want to see some pictures as well, then go to my Gallery Page.

Thursday 25th August

Arrived in Montreal, Canada, after nearly 12 hours on the plane. Slept! Felt a lot better the next morning and the hotel was really nice. Montreal is quite old and – very French! Yes, here we were in Canada and everyone was speaking French. Fortunately, most **4**_____ speak English too.

Saturday 27th August

We had hired a car for the ten days of our holiday, and on Saturday we drove south into the USA. I was really excited. We **5**_____ Saturday night in a small town called Lincoln. Everyone was so friendly – some kids outside the hotel asked me if I wanted to play baseball. When I said I was from England, they were really **6**_____ ! We talked for about half an hour.

Sunday 28th August

Drove south to Boston. I'd learned so much **7**_____ Boston in history lessons at school (the Tea Party, Independence and all that), I couldn't believe I was here now. You can **8**_____ see all the old buildings, but they're next to skyscrapers. It looked funny.

Tuesday 30th August

OK, Boston was interesting, but this was the part of the holiday I'd been really **9**_____ : New York! We arrived late afternoon and crossed the Brooklyn Bridge – the one you see in all the photos. And then there it was: skyscrapers, yellow taxis, people everywhere. The place is crazy. There **10**_____ don't seem to be any rules! Then you start to "go with the flow" and it's fantastic. I could have stayed here until the end of the holiday, but ...

Thursday 1st September

... we drove north again. Spent the night in a horrible motel in a little place called Binghamton, then on Friday drove to Buffalo and spent the day **11**_____ the Niagara Falls. Yes, the Niagara Falls! I loved it, but there were **12**_____ tourists.

Saturday 3rd September

The holiday was almost over but **13** _____ time to see just one more place before flying home.

Back in Canada, we stayed Saturday and Sunday in Toronto. It's really modern – and after the USA, it seemed clean and quiet. The most famous thing here is the CN Tower, the world's tallest building. Right at the top there's a glass floor! Scary but great **14** _____ !

On Sunday evening, we dropped off our hire car at Toronto airport and boarded our plane for London. Goodbye Canada and the States – until next time.

1
A ☐ always
B ☐ sometimes
C ☐ ever
D ☐ already

2
A ☐ begin
B ☐ become
C ☐ behave
D ☐ believe

3
A ☐ When
B ☐ After
C ☐ If
D ☐ While

4
A ☐ peoples
B ☐ people
C ☐ pupil
D ☐ personal

5
A ☐ have stopped
B ☐ stop
C ☐ were stopping
D ☐ stopped

6
A ☐ interesting
B ☐ interested
C ☐ of interest
D ☐ interest

7
A ☐ over
B ☐ about
C ☐ around
D ☐ after

8
A ☐ already
B ☐ ever
C ☐ never
D ☐ still

9
A ☐ waiting for
B ☐ waited for
C ☐ waiting after
D ☐ waited after

10
A ☐ never
B ☐ just
C ☐ always
D ☐ hardly

11
A ☐ visit
B ☐ visits
C ☐ visited
D ☐ visiting

12
A ☐ a little
B ☐ much
C ☐ lots of
D ☐ another

13
A ☐ it gave
B ☐ it had
C ☐ there was
D ☐ there is

14
A ☐ luck
B ☐ lucky
C ☐ funny
D ☐ fun

D Text production

> • *Choose one of the following tasks and write about 150 words.*
> • *Count your words and write the number at the end of the text.*

What is the story behind the picture?

> *Write a text and include at least four of the following aspects:*
> • *Who is it?*
> • *When and where is it?*
> • *How did the person get here?*
> • *What will happen next?*
> • *What are your/their thoughts?*

More sport – why don't we do it?
An online magazine has opened a discussion on the following topic:
We all know that we should do more sport. So why don't we do it?

> *Write an entry on this discussion giving your opinion and include at least four of the following aspects:*
> • *why sport is important*
> • *why some people don't like sport*
> • *other things that are good for you*
> • *your experience of different sports*
> • *your opinion on the question in the title*

Übersicht über die Aufgaben zum Hörverstehen

Die Tonaufnahmen (MP3-Dateien) und die Hörtexte findest du online unter www.scook.de. Deinen persönlichen Zugangscode findest du auf Seite 1 deines Abschlussprüfungstrainers.

Track	Kapitel	Titel	Seite
1	Training Section	Calgary's skyways (Part 1)	8
2	Training Section	Calgary's skyways (Part 2)	9
3	Training Section	Calgary's skyways (Part 3)	9
4	Training Section	Calgary's skyways (Part 4)	10
5	Training Section	Calgary's skyways (Part 5)	10
6	Training Section	The Niagara Falls (Version 1)	10
7	Training Section	The Niagara Falls (Version 2)	12
8	Training Section	The *Tour de Yorkshire*	13
9	Training Section	Bob Marley	14
10	Training Section	Top of the Rock	14
11	Musterprüfung 1	Bo-Kaap – a special district in Cape Town	44
12	Musterprüfung 1	Concorde	44
13	Musterprüfung 1	Adverts	45
14	Musterprüfung 1	A presentation about William Shakespeare	46
15	Musterprüfung 2	A report about St Kilda	57
16	Musterprüfung 2	A report about Wales	57
17	Musterprüfung 2	Radio notices	58
18	Musterprüfung 2	First job	58
19	Urheberrechtserklärung		

Studio: Clarity Studio Berlin
Regie und Aufnahmeleitung: Christian Schmitz
Tontechnik: Christian Marx, Pascal Thinius